10/25

£3.00

LONGEVITY LIFESTYLE

A Simple Program of Nutrition and Exercise For Prolonging the Prime of Your Life

LONGEVITY LIFESTYLE

A Simple Program of Nutrition and Exercise For Prolonging the Prime of Your Life

Ann Tyndall, Ph.D.

**NEWCASTLE PUBLISHING CO., INC.
NORTH HOLLYWOOD, CALIFORNIA
1986**

Copyright © 1986 by Ann Tyndall
All rights reserved
ISBN 0-87877-086-0

Edited by Hank Stine and Janrae Frank
Cover/Book design by Riley K. Smith

FIRST EDITION

A NEWCASTLE BOOK
First Printing April 1986
9 8 7 6 5 4 3 2 1
Printed in the United States of America

For Bob, the Love of my life

CONTENTS

Introduction: In Search of the Fountain of Youth   xi

I   THE BIG NUTRITION RIP-OFF   1
    The Medicine Show   1
    Grapefruit Juice, Vinegar and Rolling Pins   2
    You Can Detect Quackery   2
    Pill Power   3
    The Danger Zone   4
    C in the Sky   6
    What You Can Do   8

II   LONGEVITY LIFESTYLES   9
    The Long-Lived Peoples of the World   9
    Age Takes a Place of Honor   10
    Food for a Hundred Years   11
    Activity Level for Longevity   12
    Hypokinetic Disease   14
    Fit for Life   14
    What You Can Do   17

III   NUTRITION AND CANCER   21
    Cancer—A Lifestyle Disease?   21
    Interpretation of the Research   22
    The Biggest Dietary Culprit—Fat   22
    Vitamin A—A Cancer Inhibitor?   24
    Vitamin C and Cancer Prevention   25
    Alcohol Plus Smoking Equals Synergy   25
    Aflatoxins—Carcinogens on Grains and Peanuts   26
    Mushrooms—Better Left as Toadstools?   27
    Coffee—The Jury Is Still Out   27

　　　　Mutagens from Cooking Foods　28
　　　　Artificial Sweeteners—Are They Safe or
　　　　　Not?　28
　　　　Plastic Food Containers and Packaging　29
　　　　Good News in the Cabbage Patch　30
　　　　What You Can Do　30

IV　EATING TO EXCESS—FATS IN FOODS　33
　　　　What's Good about Fats　33
　　　　The Bad News　33
　　　　Cholesterol, the Good, the Bad and the
　　　　　Ugly　35
　　　　Polyunsaturated Fats Versus Saturated
　　　　　Fats—Is Butter Better?　37
　　　　Cis to Trans—An Unnatural Act　38
　　　　Invisible Fat　40
　　　　Fast Food Fills More than Your
　　　　　Stomach　42
　　　　What You Can Do　43

V　THE CARBOHYDRATE CONNECTION　45
　　　　Sensual Sweetness　45
　　　　The Origins of a Sweet Tooth　46
　　　　The Sugar Villains　47
　　　　Honey—A Romantic Sweet　48
　　　　Other "Virtuous" Sweets　49
　　　　Are Cereals Really Candy?　50
　　　　The Sugar-Diabetes Connection　51
　　　　Sugar and Mood Swings　51
　　　　Bad Press for Starches　53
　　　　Brantastic Benefits　54
　　　　What You Can Do　56

Table of Contents

VI THE PROTEIN MYSTIQUE — 59
- Protein—The Power Nutrient 59
- "Lose Fifteen Pounds the First Week!" 61
- Could Too Much Protein Be Dangerous? 63
- Complete Protein Without Meat 63
- Getting the Essentials 63
- Tofu 66
- Gelatin, The Protein Weakling 67
- What You Can Do 68

VII PREVENTING BONE LOSS AND OSTEOPOROSIS — 69
- "She Fell and Broke Her Hip" 69
- Building Strong Bones 70
- Calcium Intake and Fracture Risk 71
- Dietary Interactions 71
- Physical Activity and Lifestyle 72
- What You Can Do 73

VIII TOWARD LIFETIME WEIGHT CONTROL — 75
- Fat Baby, Fat Forever? 75
- The Real Cost of Obesity 76
- Why We Overeat 77
- How to Stop Recreational Eating 80
- Imagery and Visualization for a Thinner You 83
- Train Your Body to Burn More Calories 85
- Fitness for Life 88
- Environmental Support—Family and Friends 90
- What You Can Do 91

IX THE LONGEVITY DIET   95
    The Longevity Diet   97
    Calcium Group   97
    Protein Group   97
    Vegetable Group   98
    Fruit Group   100
    Complex Carbohydrate Group   101
    A Quick Guide to the Longevity Diet   102
    How to Preserve Nutrients in Foods   103
    The Sodium Story   105
    What You Can Do   107

X   LIFE ENRICHMENT AND LONGEVITY   109
    How to Get What You Want   109
    Leave Your Comfort Zone   111
    Get Rid of Energy Vampires   111
    Ways to Be Nice to Yourself   112
    The Importance of Touch   115
    What You Can Do   117

Bibliography   119

INTRODUCTION

IN SEARCH OF THE FOUNTAIN OF YOUTH

The study of aging, gerontology, is a relatively new science, though lengthening the lifespan has been a goal of human kind for centuries. The First Emperor of China offered huge rewards for anyone who could find the secret to renewed youth and prolonged life. The great magicians of Shantung cast spells, concocted potions and induced trances to lengthen life. Ponce de Leon spent his life following stories and rumors, searching for the Fountain of Youth, an enchanted pool of water that could give everlasting youth to those who drank from it. Leonardo da Vinci dissected many corpses, hoping to discover the secrets of life and death.

In their attempt to uncover these secrets researchers have begun to study the mechanism of aging. For example, what signals the cells to stop multiplying, grow old and die? Why do some people live to be ninety-five, maintaining an active life, while others begin to slow down at the age of sixty and then die of some chronic disease?

In order to answer these questions, various studies have been done on long lived people. Other studies have involved the transplantation of aging organs into young hosts to see if there was any regeneration of the organs. (There were not.) Though the lifespan of one's biological parents remains the most important predictor of one's lifespan, there have been some important findings from recent research that allow anyone to extend their lifespan many years beyond what they might normally expect. It is the purpose of this book to explore this research and make recommendations based on these findings for positive changes you can make in your lifestyle that will help to prolong the prime of your life.

For instance, recent advances in medical science have shown that the two biggest killer diseases in the United States, heart disease and cancer, are heavily influenced by lifestyle. If lifestyle plays a major part in the prevention of these diseases, then at a minimum that means we are in control of two of the major factors that influence longevity and quality of life. Following the advice given in the chapters in this book on nutrition and cancer and fats in foods could significantly reduce your chances of succumbing to heart disease or cancer.

So can exercise. Instead of a fountain of youth, perhaps it would be more accurate to say there is a mountain of youth. The peoples of the world who live the longest inhabit mountainous regions that require them to engage in a great deal of physical activity during their daily lives. Of all the populations studied, the single most important common factor influencing the subject's longevity (other than genetic inheritance) was exercise. The chapter on exercise and lifestyles outlines a program of physical activity that is designed so anyone can follow it, no matter what their current physical condition.

Did you ever wonder why you never see very old people who are over weight? There is a reason. In the chapter on fats and weight you will learn the techniques for lifetime weight control and how these habits can keep you healthier, longer.

As we grow older the risk of hip and bone fractures, as well as osteoporosis (bone loss) increases. The chapter on bones and aging recommends dietary changes and physical activity that can decrease your chances of getting osteoporosis and debilitating bone fractures.

This book focuses on nutrition as a proven key to retaining and regaining youthful vigor and extending the life span. But it is a total approach to lifestyle habits, including exercise, weight control, goal setting, and life enrichment. It was written not only for older people who are interested in maintaining their health but for younger people who can reap long-term benefits from positive health habits. Each chapter includes a section at the end, "What You Can Do," that gives practical recommendations for putting research findings into action.

There is a massive amount of misinformation and false claims about nutrition, and it is difficult to know what is the right thing to do when faced with so many conflicting choices. Some people have even become convinced that there is no way to get adequate nutritional benefits from the natural food supply; therefore, they take a variety of food supplements, but still have an uneasy feeling that something could be missing from their diet. This book will answer many of people's most frequently asked questions about what foods are healthiest and provide an easy to follow nutritional program that will help prolong the prime of your life.

Remember, knowledge is power. You *can* make informed changes that will reduce the risk of illness, add years to your lifespan and prolong the prime of your life.

CHAPTER I

THE BIG NUTRITION RIP-OFF

THE MEDICINE SHOW

In 19th Century America, the medicine show, a traveling group of entertainers, sold elixirs and potions that were supposed to cure just about anything, prolong youth, iron out wrinkles, and effortlessly melt away fat. All this may have sounded too good to be true, but many people bought these products anyway, with the vain hope that they might, indeed, contain the magic formula they promised.

In some ways, things haven't changed much. Man is still searching for the key to everlasting youth, and people still put on dazzling entertainments designed to sell products that promise amazing results. The result of all this commercial hype is a great deal of confusion about what to eat, whether to take nutrition supplements, what kind of exercise is best, how to lose weight, and how to make life longer and better. This chapter will explore some of the common misconceptions people have about these issues.

GRAPEFRUIT JUICE, VINEGAR AND ROLLING PINS

According to some, grapefruit juice and vinegar (because of their acid content) are supposed to burn off fat, no matter how much you eat. According to others, it is possible to roll off fat with a rolling pin. Logically, if grapefruit juice were a strong enough acid to eat up fat, it would probably eat up your tongue and throat, too. And if fat could really be mechanically rolled off, we would have less of it on our behinds than anywhere else. The problem is that many of us want so desperately to believe there is an easy way to lose weight that we will buy products that don't even make sense to us in the hope that they will work. Today the sale of grapefruit pills is making millions for its developer and mechanical "butt-rollers" can be found in spas and health clubs all over this country. Unfortunately, quackery thrives on conditions that are difficult or impossible to cure, such as obesity, arthritis and cancer.

With so many weight-loss, age-controlling, arthritis-curing products on the market today, how is it possible to know which ones can be trusted? Obviously, the average consumer can't look them all up in the medical journals. Without a degree in medicine or nutrition, how can you make informed choices? Following are some guidelines that will warn you if a product or diet is unsound.

YOU CAN DETECT QUACKERY

Become suspicious when you see a product that is presented in any of the following ways:

1. *Dramatic results.* "Lose ten pounds the first week." "Watch the wrinkles melt away before your eyes." "Cures arthritis in 24 hours." If it sounds too good to be true, it probably is.
2. *Superlative words* like "amazing," "super," "revolutionary new discovery," "powerful."
3. *Scientific-sounding words* (to impress you) like "cellulite," "fat-mobilizing hormone," "lecithin," "lipases."
4. *Testimonials* of people who have tried the product. Claims based on research that has been tested on large samples of people are better indications of a sound product than the endorsements of a few.
5. *Claims to be a cure-all.* This is probably the most dangerous claim of all because it can prevent people from getting the medical attention they need. There is no food, vitamin, diet, pill or device that is an actual cure-all.
6. *Claims the seller is persecuted* by the medical association because doctors are afraid of the competition.
7. *A diet that emphasizes one food*, such as the banana diet or one that leaves out entire food groups, such as the high-protein diet, which omits breads, cereals and other complex carbohydrates.

PILL POWER

There is a natural order of things on the earth. The sun rises in the east, objects fall down instead of up, and our bodies function optimally when nourished by food. Pill pushers and "nutrition" magazines (supported by ads for vitamin pills and food supplements) have led the public to believe that our food supply is leached of its nutrients while they leach us of our money by selling overpriced, grossly overrated food supplements. The fact is, the American food supply is the safest and the healthiest in the world. While there *are* many synthetic food products on the market that offer only recreational value, it is still possible to select a highly nutritious diet from the average supermarket.

Many misguided consumers today spend $100–200 per month on food supplements and vitamin pills. The truth is an average month's supply of the vitamins most commonly found in supplements is worth less than six cents. It is interesting to note that vitamins, essential nutrients for life, originated in food (and food is still the best source), yet many people think that the primary source of vitamins today is to be found in a pill bottle. We would all get far greater value for our money (and our bodies) if we would spend that money on nutritious food instead of on useless food supplements.

THE DANGER ZONE

Although vitamins are essential to life, the body has no use for excess vitamins. In fact, vitamin deficiency diseases are rarely seen in the United States, but due to successful media indoctrination many people feel that to be on the "safe side" they should still supplement their diets with vitamin pills.

Many ill-informed consumers believe that if a little of a vitamin is good for you, then a lot must be even better. This is the beginning of the mega-dose mentality in which individuals may take 50–200 times as much of a vitamin as their body needs. This is possible only with vitamin supplements since no one could possibly consume dosages that large by eating food alone.

For example, some people take as much as 1500 International Units (IU) a day of Vitamin E, a fat-soluble vitamin that can be stored in the body. The Recommended Dietary Allowance (RDA) is 30 IU a day. That is 50 times as much as the body can use, and if you were to try to eat its equivalent in food, it would take eight or nine pounds of vegetable oil (a rich food source of Vitamin E) to supply that amount!

What does the body do with this excess? If it is a fat-soluble vitamin, as Vitamins A, D, E and K are, the body stores it. Since some vitamins are more harmful in large amounts than others, taking megadoses of them over a prolonged period of time could put you in danger of an overdose. For example, taking ten times the recommended daily dosage of either Vitamin A or D for even one month has been reported to have toxic effects, resulting in skin abnormalities, vision problems, and liver damage.

Though the effects of high doses of Vitamin E are not as serious as those of Vitamins A and D, one can easily see that it is unnatural, if not harmful, to have such extreme excess levels of a nutrient in the body. It is practically impossible to get an overdose of a vitamin just from eating food. If you want to be sure of getting enough Vitamin E, it is abundant in many food sources, such as wheat germ, whole grain breads and cereals, fruits, and green vegetables.

No matter what the actual facts, some people insist on taking a vitamin/mineral supplement that provides several times more than 100% of the RDA, compared to those providing the actual daily requirement. Keep in mind that some fortified cereals provide 100% of the RDA of most vitamins and minerals and are the equivalent of taking a vitamin pill.

For best absorption, vitamin supplements should be taken with meals, since food is the best source of nutrients and contains the necessary compounds to facilitate absorption. For example, calcium is best absorbed in the presence of lactic acid, which is found in milk, and iron is best absorbed in the presence of Vitamin C, which is found in some fruits and vegetables.

Contrary to what many people think, there is no difference in quality or absorbability between synthetic vitamins and natural vitamins. Vitamins are chemical compounds and their molecular configuration is the same whether they were manufactured in the laboratory or squeezed from a plant, separated and dehydrated. Since scientists are discovering new things in the field of nutrition every day, it is likely that there are many other undiscovered compounds in food that aid us in absorbing vitamins. This was demonstrated by a study in which rats were fed exclusively on food supplements that contained all the known essential nutrients. After a period of time, the rats' tails fell off, and they died. This is a reminder that it is not a good idea to rely heavily on vitamins and other food supplements for nutrition because they do not contain everything that is essential to sustaining life.

C IN THE SKY

When Linus Pauling came out with the book, *Vitamin C and the Common Cold*, millions of Americans began taking large doses of Vitamin C. His findings suggested that taking megadoses of Vitamin C every day resulted in people contracting fewer colds, and even those colds were of less severity and shorter duration than normal. That study has since been repeated by many researchers and it still has not been confirmed. However, as a result of Pauling's book, many people began routinely taking megadoses of Vitamin C.

The RDA for Vitamin C is 30 milligrams, about the amount which one-third of a cup of orange juice provides. Some people were taking 500 milligrams (mg) of C four times a day, resulting in an intake of 2000 mg, or 67 times as much as the body needs! The body's tissues become saturated at an intake of 100 milligrams. Intakes over that amount are wasted and the excess is passed out of the body in the urine.

That seems harmless enough, but it has been found that at megadose levels, the body adapts to the higher intake and begins to require it. If the individual then suddenly stops taking high levels of Vitamin C, they may experience symptoms of scurvy (bleeding gums, bruising easily, and wounds which fail to heal). This was first discovered in the cases of infants whose mothers had taken megadoses of C. The infants developed signs of scurvy on a normal diet, after having adapted to high levels of C while in the mother's womb. If someone has been taking large amounts of C and decides to cut down on the amount, they should do it gradually.

In all the publicity over Pauling's research into the relationship between Vitamin C and the prevention of colds, one vital detail failed to make an impact on the public. The best results were obtained in studies where the subjects consumed their Vitamin C in the form of oranges and orange juice rather than in supplements.

WHAT YOU CAN DO

1. *Follow the guidelines in this chapter* as you evaluate new diets, techniques and products for health promotion.
2. *Avoid taking more than 100% of the RDA* in vitamin/mineral supplements. If you are now taking megadoses of Vitamin C, gradually reduce your consumption to no more than 100% of the RDA. If you are taking large doses of Vitamins A, D, E, or K, stop immediately.
3. *Become mindful of nutritious foods* and think of ways that your diet could be healthier. The chapters that follow will give you hundreds of suggestions for ways to make positive changes.

CHAPTER II

LONGEVITY LIFESTYLES

THE LONG-LIVED PEOPLES OF THE WORLD

Certain areas scattered throughout the world—the highlands of Georgia in the Soviet Union, Vilcabamba, Ecuador, and Hunza, West Pakistan—have an unusually large proportion of people who live to be over 100 years old (centenarians). These individuals, even in their seventies, eighties and nineties, are extraordinarily active and involved with the pleasures and challenges of life. Though there have been exaggerated claims for longevity in these areas, with some claiming to be up to 160 years old, there are few official records to substantiate these claims. The longest-lived person of whose age we have documented proof was Delina Filkins of Herkimer County, New York, who lived to be almost 114 years old.

Scientists have done considerable research to determine what factors are responsible for the unusual longevity of these people. While it is true that genetic inheritance plays a key role in longevity, it was found that when people from long-lived families were moved from their traditional environment into the city, they began to die at the same rate as other urban citizens. This suggests that, in some cases, environment may be as influential as genetic inheritance on longevity. Now that modern science has conquered most of the infectious killer diseases, we are primarily dying of "lifestyle diseases," maladies that are precipitated or worsened by sedentary and indulgent habits. With this in mind, we can learn a great deal by investigating the eating patterns, exercise habits, personality traits and personal relationships of the long-lived peoples of the world.

Most of these peoples live in cool, mountainous regions, with clean air and water, and a slower pace of life than citydwellers experience. Few ever stopped working as they grew older, though they began to work fewer hours than before (four to five hours a day). Most of them did manual labor on the farm and claimed that they enjoyed physical exertion, though they refrained from working to exhaustion. They all walked several miles a day. Many rode horses, chopped wood, hauled water, danced, and bathed in mountain streams, even at the most advanced ages. The majority of these people were married, though some had had two or three spouses. Very few of those studied smoked, but many of them enjoyed alcohol in moderation every day (three or four ounces of wine or one or two ounces of vodka).

AGE TAKES A PLACE OF HONOR

In the Abkhasian group, in the Soviet Union, individuals actually look forward to growing old because of the honor and recognition it brings. The elderly participate in every aspect of society, presiding at many official and social functions, serving as arbiters in family, village, and regional councils and often performing musical and dance pieces at social gatherings. Even if an elder is sick, his counsel is still sought and there is no evidence of any "generation gap."

The Soviet authorities have established a Council of Elders in each village to serve as an advisory council to the government. The elders are consulted first before any changes are made. However, the women acquire equality with men only after menopause, and at that time are allowed to participate in decisions.

In every village there is a chorus of musicians which only those who are 70 years or older are allowed to join. It is a great honor to be a part of this chorus and the elders derive obvious pleasure from practicing and performing their music.

The apparent connection between these peoples' longevity and their level of leadership and social involvement indicates that if we want to cultivate longevity in our own society, many of our present attitudes toward aging and the old must change. The predominant view of the elderly in this country—where those over 65 are removed from the mainstream of life—needs to be re-examined.

FOOD FOR A HUNDRED YEARS

Another major factor in the lives of most of those who became centenarians was their eating habits. Their diet was lower in calories than the American diet, averaging 1500 to 2000 calories a day, compared to the American average of 3000 to 4000. This was reflected in the lean body composition of the subjects studied.

Most of the food eaten (70%) was vegetables and dairy products. The remainder was fruits, nuts and grains. Meat was rarely consumed and when it was, it was eaten in small amounts, perhaps more as a garnish (as in Oriental food) than as a main course. The world's long-lived peoples consumed very little coffee, tea or sugar, and only small amounts of butter and salt. The Abkhasians, for instance, insisted on freshness and picked their vegetables just before cooking.

Numerous studies show vegetarian groups have a lifespan of five to ten years longer than meat-eating groups. Those on vegetarian or low-meat diets have extremely low rates of hypertension, hyperglycemia and hypoglycemia, while those on diets that were high in beef content had the highest incidence of cancer, particularly of the breast and colon.

Alcohol, in moderation, has been correlated with longer life. Individuals who drank one-half liter of wine a day (about two glasses) lived longer than those who drank more or did not drink at all. Alcohol relieves stress, stimulates the appetite and stimulates the production of high-density lipoproteins, which return fat from the arterial walls to the heart (a benefit). There will be more about this in the chapter on fats.

ACTIVITY LEVEL FOR LONGEVITY

Though the geographical locations of the groups studied are diverse, one factor that all members have in common is that they continued a physically active lifestyle almost to the moment of their deaths. Most did physically demanding work and walked a great deal. Some actually ran. The Tarahumara Indians of northern Mexico actually spend most of their time running deer or pursuing leisure activities that require running, such as foot races and other endurance sports. The Tarahumara hunters, whose members live into their nineties, can chase a deer for days until the deer drops from exhaustion or is run over a cliff.

Exercise has also been found to reduce blood cholesterol. The cholesterol levels of some centenarians in the Soviet Union was 98, compared with 250, an upper normal for a middle-aged American. Members of the Masai tribe of Africa, who consume a diet high in cholesterol (beef, blood of cattle and whole milk dairy products) do not have elevated cholesterol levels, probably due to their active lifestyle. The Masai walk up to 20 miles a day while tending their herds.

Researchers found that exercise is also related to reducing the risk of heart disease. In a study that compared bus-drivers and ticket-takers on double-decker buses, significantly more cases of heart disease were found among the drivers (who were sedentary) than among the ticket-takers (who walked up and down the bus all day). Another study compared Irish-American city workers who drove to work with their brothers in Ireland who rode bicycles to agricultural jobs. The more active brothers in Ireland had a lower incidence of heart disease.

A number of studies have been done to determine if athletes live longer than their sedentary counterparts. These studies have demonstrated that a program of 20–50 minutes of aerobic physical activity three to five times a week lowers blood cholesterol and plasma triglycerides, reduces blood pressure, lowers resting heart rate and total body fat. All of these favorably affect longevity by reducing the risk of heart disease.

The studies also showed that these positive benefits continue only while the person engages in regular physical activity. If they change over to a sedentary lifestyle, then they stand just as much chance of getting heart disease as someone who has been inactive all their life. In other words, you cannot "store up" health benefits in youth to enjoy at a later age.

HYPOKINETIC DISEASE

Kraus and Raab, who studied the effects of insufficient activity levels on the human body, concluded that lack of exercise can cause "hypokinetic disease" (an increased incidence of cardiovascular disease, hypertension, low back pain, decline of muscular strength and endurance, and stiffening of the joints). Antigravity muscles weaken, giving a humpback appearance and restricting respiratory movements.

For instance, bedrest can result in decreased lean body mass and decreased aerobic capacity. One study of healthy college athletes showed a significant loss of muscle mass and aerobic capacity after just one week of bed rest. It took them more than one month to regain the fitness level they had attained before. It seems conclusive that adequate physical activity is essential for health and necessary for preserving body functions.

FIT FOR LIFE

Almost half of our adult population does not engage in a regular program of purposeful, non-job related physical activity and most of that half are older adults. When researchers asked why they were so sedentary, the majority said they had thought they *were* getting enough exercise. In actuality most of them were not getting their heart rate ten beats higher than what it had been during sleep.

Many older people feel that their daily routine gives them all the exercise they need. To get significant cardiovascular benefits, the heart rate needs to be elevated to about 60 percent above normal for twenty to fifty minutes a day. This should be practiced three to five times a week.

A major barrier to exercise for older adults is their feeling that it is too late for them to begin, plus their fear of injury. Several studies have shown that older adults who have been sedentary all their lives can start a successful program of physical activity, with benefits similar to those achieved in younger age groups. Reducing the risk of heart disease, among other factors. Below are some of the benefits of a regular fitness program (emphasizing walking as the predominant activity) which can help to significantly lengthen your life span:

1. Increased cardiovascular fitness, reducing the risk of heart disease.

2. Increased strength. Men and women lose 20 percent of their strength between the ages of 30 and 65. Exercise can help to maintain strength throughout life. Several studies have shown significant strength gains in elderly subjects who participated in a regular exercise program.

3. Increased flexibility. There is a decrease in flexibility from childhood through old age. Individuals who are 60 years old are ten times stiffer than those who are 10. Increased flexibility is the quickest benefit to show up after beginning an exercise program with results becoming evident in only two or three weeks.

4. Change in body composition from fat to leaner body tissue. Muscle tissue converts to fat as a natural process of aging. This reduces the basal metabolic rate, causing the person to require fewer calories to maintain their weight. Many older people continue to eat the same amount as they always did and gain weight. Increasing one's activity level prevents some of the conversion of muscle mass to fat, burns more calories and helps to keep the basal metabolic rate higher.

5. Increased bone density. Beginning around the age of 35, the body begins to lose bone tissue and if this continues at a rapid rate, it can result in osteoporosis, a condition of porous, brittle bones. Increasing one's physical activity forces the body to make denser bone to withstand the mechanical force of the exercise. This effect was demonstrated in tennis players where the bone in the tennis arm was found to be more dense than in the other arm.

   Increased bone density reduces the risk of osteoporosis (there will be more about this in a later chapter). It is important to note that only exercises which involve mechanical force, such as walking, running, tennis and, to some extent, cycling, have this effect. Swimming, an excellent exercise for cardiovascular fitness and good for people who are prone to injury, does not produce the mechanical force effect.

6. Lower stress levels. Physical exercise increases brain endorphin, a natural pain killer and tranquilizer that is more potent than morphine. A regular fitness program has been shown to lower stress levels repeatedly in all age groups studied.

7. Better sleep patterns. As one ages, sleep patterns become more erratic with the period of deep sleep becoming shorter, REM sleep (rapid eye movement sleep with dreaming which has been shown to reduce stress) decreases, and there are more episodes of awakening during the night. Exercise promotes better sleep patterns, affecting all of these factors.

8. Regular bowel movements. Exercise promotes intestinal motility, increasing regularity.

9. Enhanced self-image. A regular fitness program gives a person a greater feeling of control in their life. Personality tests have shown that individuals have increased self-confidence and enhance self-image with regular exercise.

WHAT YOU CAN DO

1. *If you are over the age of 35, check with your physician* to see if it is advisable for you to begin a program of increased physical activity.

2. *Consult the table below* to determine what your training heart rate is. The training heart rate is the heart rate per minute you need to reach and maintain for a minimum of 20 minutes a day for maximum fitness benefits.

Training Heart Rates (HR)

Age	HR	Age	HR
20	180	50	140
30	166	60	128
40	152	70	118

These rates are averages and there are many differences between individuals depending on beginning fitness level and body size. You may want to begin at a lower level than is suggested in this chart if you have a large body build or are particularly out of shape.

Take care not to overexert. If you feel extremely out of breath, dizzy or feel pressure on your chest or chest pain, stop immediately. A good guideline to follow is not to exercise so hard that you are too out of breath to talk.

3. *Begin a walking program* in which you monitor your heart rate by taking your pulse every ten minutes. Walk or run briskly enough to get your heart rate into the training range (as indicated in the table above). Continue walking (or running) at this rate for 20 to 50 minutes a day. Repeat three to five times a week.

4. *Increase physical activity.* Buy a pedometer (you can find one in most athletic stores), and find out how many miles you walk a day, during your normal activities. Most people average around three miles a day. Each mile you walk burns about 100 calories. Try to gradually increase your distance to around six miles or more a day. You may do this with planned walking periods, parking further from your destination and walking part of the way, or doing more leisure activities that require walking, such as tennis, bowling, golf, dancing (square dancing is good).

The best aerobic activities for total fitness are:

walking or running
hiking in hilly terrain
cycling
cross-country skiing
swimming
dancing strenuously
digging, hoeing or raking
shoveling snow
splitting logs or sawing wood
rowing
walking up and down stairs

All these activities burn from 300–500 calories an hour.

5. *Find activities you enjoy* that fit into your lifestyle. Many people enjoy a group setting, joining a spa and participating in aerobic classes. Others find this doesn't fit their schedules or personal preference. But it is helpful to have someone to walk/run with, particularly in the beginning. After your habits are established, it may be easier to do them on your own.

6. *Set goals for yourself.* When will you begin? Today? Write down enjoyable ways that you can increase your level of physical activity. Do you like to walk on the beach, at the park, in the mountains? Would taking dancing lessons be a fun thing to do with a special person? Is it time to do some yard work or begin a garden? Who would you like to begin this program with?

7. *Do stretching and warm-ups* before beginning any kind of exercise. There are numerous books and tapes that give instructions for how to begin. With age, it is increasingly important to have an adequate warm-up and cool-down period to prevent injuries. For example, walk slowly at the beginning of the exercise program before walking fast or running. Cool down by walking at the end of the exercise period. Never stop abruptly after a vigorous exercise session because your body needs time to readjust to the slower pace and regulate your heartbeat accordingly.

8. *Change your eating habits* and adopt a program similar to that described in the section, "Food for a Hundred Years." The chapter, "Longevity Diet" will give you details on how to implement these changes.

CHAPTER III

NUTRITION AND CANCER

CANCER—A LIFESTYLE DISEASE?

About one-fifth of all deaths in the United States are caused by cancer. It is this country's second biggest killer, with heart disease being number one. A recent article in the *Journal of the National Cancer Institute* stated that approximately 40% of the cancers in men and 60% of the cancers in women could be attributed to dietary factors. It also stated that though a change in diet may not produce immediate dramatic effects, over time, proper diet could result in a 35% overall reduction in an individual's risk of cancer. Research has shown that most cancers have external causes and could, therefore, be preventable. This became evident when blacks and Japanese who migrated to the United States, instead of developing the kind of cancers predominant in their countries, developed cancers typical for the U.S. population.

In general, some types of diets and foods tend to increase the risk of cancer, whereas others tend to decrease it. High-fat diets, and frequent consumption of salt-cured, salt-pickled and smoked foods increases the risk of cancer. Low-fat diets, predominantly vegetarian, and frequent consumption of certain fruits and vegetables decrease the cancer risk.

INTERPRETATION OF THE RESEARCH

It is difficult to prove that a given diet or food causes cancer in humans because, for ethical reasons, it is impossible to do the research on humans. As a result, most cancer research is done on animals or is what is called epidemiological research. In epidemiological research, scientists record the eating habits of people who have cancer and compare them with the eating habits of those of the same age who did not contract cancer. In edpidemiological research, one might find, for example, that individuals who contracted bladder cancer drank more coffee than those individuals who were cancer free. Such a finding does not mean that coffee drinking causes bladder cancer, only that it is related to it. We cannot determine cause and effect in such a study because there are so many factors—such as drinking water, air quality, drug ingestion, heredity, etc.—that cannot be controlled. That is one reason why animal research is necessary so often—with animals we can control and measure those factors.

While science cannot yet prescribe a foolproof diet that will prevent cancer, it has identified certain dietary factors that greatly influence the body's ability to ward off the formation of cancer and to inhibit its growth.

THE BIGGEST DIETARY CULPRIT—FAT

The Committee on Diet, Nutrition, and Cancer of the National Research Council has stated that:

> Of all the dietary components studied, the combined epidemiological and experimental evi-

dence is most suggestive for a causal relationship between fat intake and the occurrence of cancer . . . There is convincing evidence that increasing the intake of total fat increases the incidence of cancer at certain sites, particularly the breast and colon, and, conversely, that the risk is lower with lower intakes of fat.

Animals who consumed fewer calories also had a longer lifespan and fewer cases of cancer.

It was also found that polyunsaturated fats promoted cancer more than saturated fats. From this evidence, it appears that the first goal of dietary change should be to reduce total fat intake. Then for the small amount of added fat that we do consume, it should be butter instead of margarine that we use. There will be more about this in the chapter on fats and in the Longevity Diet.

The average American diet consists of approximately 40% fat. A conservative goal for fat reduction would be to reduce one's total fat intake to 30% of one's daily diet, as recommended by the American Dietary Guidelines. This recommendation was made not because it was the optimum intake of fat for prolonged health, but because it seemed to be an attainable goal for the American population.

The National Research Council suggests that a greater reduction may be even more effective as a cancer preventive. It is possible, with good planning, to reduce total fat intake to 15–20% of total calories consumed. This is more in line with the fat intake of groups that had an overall lower incidence of cancer. The chapter on the Longevity Diet will give practical suggestions for ways to reduce total fat intake and still enjoy a variety of delicious foods.

VITAMIN A—A CANCER INHIBITOR?

Of all the vitamins studied, Vitamin A has been of greatest interest to cancer researchers. As a result of a study comparing the diets of men with lung cancer with those who did not have lung cancer, it was thought to play a protective role against cancer. That study revealed that subjects who had lung cancer had generally eaten a diet that was low in Vitamin A, while those who were cancer free ate a diet that contained plenty of green, leafy vegetables and deep yellow vegetables (high in Vitamin A). Later studies showed similar results with patients who had cancer of the larynx, bladder, esophagus, stomach, colon/rectum, and prostate.

With this information, it would be tempting to take Vitamin A supplements in the hope that they would help prevent cancer, but that approach has its drawbacks. There are over 1500 different molecular configurations of Vitamin A and there would be no way to be sure which might be the right one. Also, the studies investigated vegetable consumption, not vitamin pills, and it is possible that the protective effect is from beta carotene (a precurser of Vitamin A) and/or a combination of other dietary components in food yet to be discovered.

Since Vitamin A is stored in the body, nutritionists have taught that we need to consume a rich source of it about twice a week. Based on this research, I would suggest that we need at least one serving of these foods every day. It could do no harm, and may be very beneficial. The Longevity Diet will have a list of Vitamin A-rich foods.

Liver is very high in Vitamin A but I do not recommend it. The liver is the organ for detoxification and it may contain pesticides, high levels of animal hormones, antibiotics from animal feeds and various other undesirable elements. When there are so many other foods to choose from, there is no reason to take chances with liver.

VITAMIN C AND CANCER PREVENTION

In studies done on people who ate fruits and vegetables instead of food supplements, Vitamin C (in food) has been shown to inhibit cancer of the stomach and the esophagus. An important action of Vitamin C is to block the conversion of nitrite (found in cured meats, such as bacon, ham, lunch meats, and hot dogs) to nitrosamines, a potent carcinogen (cancer promoter). For example, if you eat bacon, drink some orange juice with it. If you have ham for dinner, eat one-half of a green pepper in your salad (or a tomato). You will get more suggestions for this later. The important thing is that since your body does not store Vitamin C, you must consume a source of it every day, and if you eat cured meats, always have some Vitamin C at the same time.

There have been some studies where patients in the later stages of cancer were given Vitamin C supplements. The results were conflicting, with some patients improving, while others did not. On the whole, there was not enough evidence to suggest that Vitamin C treatments be given routinely to patients with terminal cancer.

ALCOHOL PLUS SMOKING EQUALS SYNERGY

Synergy is the cooperative action of two agents in which the combined effect is greater than the sum of the effects of the two agents taken independently. For example, excessive consumption of alcohol increases the risk of cancer of the mouth, the larynx and the esophagus. International studies have shown that excessive beer drinking is associated with cancer of the colon and the rectum. Alcohol consumers are often smokers. Of all the variables studied, smoking has been shown to be most suspect for increasing cancer risk, particularly in the respiratory tract, the mouth and the pharynx. When an individual combines smoking with drinking alcohol, they produce a synergistic effect, in that the risk of cancer is higher than the sum of the two individual risks.

For those seeking a prolonged life, a wise recommendation would be to not smoke, and if you do, don't drink alcohol, too. If you drink alcohol, use it in moderation. One study showed that cancer of the mouth was increased in individuals with poor dental health, so good dental hygiene would be a recommended cancer preventive.

AFLATOXINS—CARCINOGENS ON GRAINS AND PEANUTS

Aflatoxins are in molds that grow on grains, nuts, and peanuts and are mostly found in the southeastern United States where the climate is warm and humid. They are potent carcinogens, associated with liver cancer. There are governmental regulations controlling the levels of aflatoxin found in the food supply. In home production and storage of food, look for mold on sweet potatoes, pecans, walnuts, peanuts and corn and discard any food that looks suspicious.

Aflatoxins are most often found in corn and peanuts. You

can test cornmeal at home by looking at it under an ultraviolet light. If there are flecks in it that look shiny and iridescent green, then you should report the fact if you bought the cornmeal commercially or discard it if you produced it at home. (Take it to your local Agricultural Extension Service or call the State Department of Agriculture to report it.) *Do not eat it!*

MUSHROOMS—BETTER LEFT AS TOADSTOOLS?

Mushrooms contain hydrazines, a chemical that has been shown to cause cancer of the liver and blood vessels in rats, mice and hamsters. Though no studies have been done in humans, it may be wise not to eat mushrooms every day and particularly not to eat raw mushrooms.

COFFEE—THE JURY IS STILL OUT

Coffee has been associated with elevated risk for bladder cancer in several studies, although other studies produced conflicting results. Coffee has also been associated with an increased risk of pancreatic cancer. Drinking decaffeinated coffee does not alleviate the problem, since similar results were found in drinkers of both regular and decaffeinated coffee. Though it may be difficult (and probably unnecessary) for many people to give up coffee completely, it is probably unwise to consume massive amounts, such as five or more cups a day. Perhaps, to err on the side of safety, coffee consumption should be limited to two cups or less per day until more definite information is available.

MUTAGENS FROM COOKING FOODS

The birth of a cancer (cancer initiation) may involve alteration of the genetic material; therefore, anything that alters the DNA in the cell (mutation) could be a possible cause of cancer. Mutagens, substances that can alter DNA, can result from cooking foods. Beef grilled over a gas or charcoal fire produces mutagens when the fat from the meat drips onto the coals, therefore, meats with the highest fat content are most mutagenic when cooked over an open flame. Mutagens are also produced when foods are smoked and deep fried. Almost any kind of burned food can produce mutagens, including burned toast and other baked goods that are over-browned. It would be a good idea not to eat large quantities of these foods.

Some foods have been shown to reduce the activity of certain mutagens and these foods include cabbage, broccoli, green pepper, eggplant, apple, pineapple, ginger, shallot, lettuce, parsley, brussels sprouts, mustard greens, spinach, and other vegetables. If you do eat foods prepared on the grill, smoked, or deep-fried, include some foods that reduce mutagen activity in the same meal.

ARTIFICIAL SWEETENERS—ARE THEY SAFE OR NOT?

Several studies have linked both saccharin and cyclamates to bladder cancer. Since saccharin is an important sweetner for diabetics and, until recently, there was no satisfactory substitute for it, the Food and Drug Association allowed it to stay on the market with a warning label that said saccharin had been shown to produce cancer in laboratory animals.

Saccharin is used extensively by people who want to reduce their caloric intake and it may be overused in some cases. For example, if the pattern in humans follows the one seen in animals, an expectant mother using saccharin to help control her weight during pregnancy, may be putting future generations at risk of developing bladder cancer. Overzealous saccharin consumers may sweeten the family's tea with it and encourage their children to drink saccharin-sweetened drinks and to chew saccharin-sweetened gum to cut down on cavities that could be caused by too much sugar. The long-term effects of a child's daily consumption of saccharin have not been determined but it seems unwise to take a risk when there are other alternatives available. Sugar is less harmful than saccharin and efforts should be made to encourage children to drink more fruit juices, water and milk rather than to rely solely on artificially sweetened beverages. Perhaps saccharin has a place in the diet for the diabetic but I would not recommend it for routine consumption by normal, healthy people.

Aspartame, a new artificial sweetener, was approved in 1981 as a sweetener in certain foods. Numerous studies have been done on it and so far there is no evidence that links it to increased cancer risk.

PLASTIC FOOD CONTAINERS AND PACKAGING

Vinyl chloride is a potent carcinogen, associated with cancers of the liver, brain, respiratory tract, and lymphatic system. Containers made of polyvinyl chloride are widely used in packaging and storing foods and vinyl chloride has been found in the foods stored in them. Some foods that have been found to contain vinyl chloride are cooking oils, margarine and butter, vinegar and a variety of alcoholic beverages.

The average consumer may want to become aware of foods that are packaged in plastic containers and possibly make choices for other alternatives. For example, you may want to select cooking oils that are stored in glass containers instead of plastic. You may want to consider using less plastic wrap that comes in direct contact with the food, substituting wax paper. Use more glass storage containers and less plastic.

GOOD NEWS IN THE CABBAGE PATCH

Several studies have indicated that vegetables in the cabbage family, such as cabbage, brussels sprouts, broccoli, and cauliflower have a protective effect against cancer. It is not known exactly what it is in these foods that gives the protective effect, but it seems to work. Based on this evidence, I would recommend that individuals consume at least one serving from this group every day. These vegetables are low in calories and are a good source of vitamins and fiber, as well as possessing cancer preventative qualities.

WHAT YOU CAN DO

1. *Reduce fat in the diet.* Avoid fried foods, eat less meat and fewer high-fat snacks, such as chips, peanuts, cookies and ice cream.
2. *Eat a source of Vitamin A every day.* Choose from green leafy vegetables (spinach, turnip greens,

mustard greens, kale, collards), carrots, sweet potatoes, pumpkin, broccoli, apricots, cantalope, peaches, watermelon, and winter squash.

3. *Eat a source of Vitamin C every day.* Choose from cantalope, grapefruit, oranges, papaya, strawberries, broccoli, raw cabbage (slaw), cauliflower, collards, peppers, spinach, tomatoes, and turnip greens. You will notice that several foods are rich in both Vitamins A and C.

4. *If you drink, do so in moderation, and do not smoke.*

5. *Avoid any moldy food* (unless it is bleu cheese).

6. *Don't eat peanut butter or products made from cornmeal every day.*

7. *Consume mushrooms in moderation*, if at all, and avoid raw mushrooms.

8. *Limit coffee consumption to two cups or less per day.*

9. *Avoid deep-fried foods* and limit consumption of grilled and smoked foods. Don't eat the burned parts of any food (including burned toast).

10. *Limit consumption of cured meats*, such as bacon, ham, lunch meats, and hot dogs. If you do eat these, have a source of vitamin C with it at the same meal.

11. *Limit consumption of artificial sweeteners.*

12. *As much as possible, avoid plastic food containers and plastic wrap* that comes in direct contact with the food.

13. *Consume at least one serving of vegetables in the cabbage family every day*, such as cabbage, brussels sprouts, broccoli, or cauliflower.

CHAPTER IV

EATING TO EXCESS: FATS IN FOODS

WHAT'S GOOD ABOUT FATS

We hear a great deal about the harm that fat can do but we seldom hear about the beneficial qualities of fat. Fat is essential to our bodies and it performs many important functions including insulation of the body from extremes of temperature, providing padding to protect the internal organs, and providing the oils that give our skin a radiant complexion and make our hair glossy. The fat embedded in our muscles provides energy when we are active and fats are important components of many hormones and other essential body substances.

Fat enhances the flavor of food and is often the flavor carrier in foods, making our food taste more satisfying. It is also necessary for proper metabolism of the fat-soluble vitamins, A, D, E, and K.

THE BAD NEWS

The bad news about fat is simply that we can get too much of it. When that happens, we become overweight, run a higher risk of getting heart disease and some forms of cancer and of incurring a number of other undesirable conditions.

The average American diet is composed of 40–45% fat. The U.S. Dietary Guidelines suggest that 30% should be the goal for us to shoot for, but the National Research Council advises that a further reduction would be better, though they do not give precise guidelines. The fat content of the diets of long-lived groups was found to be 10–15%. This chapter will suggest practical ways to reduce fat in your diet and be on the way to a healthier style of eating.

Fat is the highest in calories of all the foods we eat. It has nine calories per gram and is twice as fattening as carbohydrates or protein. Many common foods are high in fat content, such as breakfast meats, luncheon meats, fast foods, chips, nuts, well-marbled steaks, fried foods, most cakes, cookies, pastries and most convenience foods. Anyone who eats very many foods from the above list runs a great risk of becoming overweight, among other hazards.

In addition, too much fat in the diet can cause an accumulation of fat in the blood vessels, resulting in hardening of the arteries. The fat mixes with blood and collagen (a protein constituent of white fibrous connective tissue), becomes waxy and sticks to the arterial walls and eventually could block the blood flow. If this happens in an artery in the heart, the result is a heart attack. If the blockage occurs in the brain, the result is a stroke.

Heart disease is this nation's number one killer and many medical authorities believe that it is a lifestyle-related disease, and that we may be able to prevent it with lifestyle modification. Of course, there are many risk factors associated with heart disease: heredity, sex (men are more at risk), lack of exercise, smoking, obesity, high blood pressure, diabetes, high blood cholesterol, and stress. No one can control their genetic inheritance, but we can control our diet, our weight, activity patterns, smoking choices, and how we handle stress. Positive lifestyle changes can make a significant impact on high blood pressure, and blood lipid levels.

CHOLESTEROL—THE GOOD, THE BAD AND THE UGLY

The good news is that there are several kinds of cholesterol (a fatty substance in the blood) in the body and one kind, called high density lipoprotein (HDL) may actually be protective against heart disease. Long-lived peoples have higher levels of HDL than those who die from heart attacks. Instead, heart attack victims are usually found to have a high level of low density lipoprotein (LDL) in their blood.

LDL is the blood lipid that seems to be associated with heart disease. LDLs supply the cells with cholesterol, thus depositing cholesterol along the way. HDLs remove cholesterol from the cells and return it to the liver.

Now we know that it is not only the total blood cholesterol level that is important in predicting heart disease risk, but the ratio of HDL to LDL. The optimum balance would be to have a higher ratio of HDL to LDL, and there are some diet patterns and lifestyle habits that promote higher levels of HDL.

As you read the following summary, remember that it is HDL that you want to increase and LDL that you want to decrease.

1. Diets that are mostly vegetarian and are high in grains, fish, fruits and vegetables raise HDL.

2. Several studies have revealed an effect that is not well understood, but whole milk, though it contains butterfat (and cholesterol) does not raise blood cholesterol and it may lower it. This effect has been called the "milk factor" and is good news for all who need to keep their milk intake up to encourage bone density. (This does not imply that everyone should drink whole milk instead of skim milk. Skim milk has the same cholesterol-lowering effect, contains less fat and is lower in calories.)
3. Moderate amounts of eggs (one a day) may be better for us than was once thought. Eggs are very nutritious, and, though high in cholesterol, have not been shown to raise blood cholesterol levels if eaten in moderation.
4. Losing weight lowers total cholesterol and raises HDL.
5. Regular exercise lowers total cholesterol and raises HDL.
6. Pectin, found in apples and other fruits, lowers total cholesterol.
7. Oatmeal has been shown to lower total cholesterol.
8. Most oral contraceptives increase LDLs and decrease HDLs.
9. Smoking increases LDLs.
10. Drinking alcohol increases HDLs. Alcoholics seldom die of heart disease. (They die more from liver disease, cancer and automobile accidents.)
11. The level of LDL is also directly related to the consumption of cholesterol and saturated fats; therefore, diets high in cholesterol and saturated fat increase LDL.

Cholesterol is only present in animal foods such as meats, fish, poultry, eggs, and whole milk dairy products. By far, the foods highest in cholesterol are the organ meats with brains the highest at a whopping 1810 mg for three ounces, followed by chicken liver at 480 mg and beef, calf and lamb liver at 373 mg. Eggs have 240 mg each. Beef, lamb, pork, veal and the dark meat of chicken and turkey all have about 80 mg of cholesterol per three-ounce serving.

The average American consumes about 600 mg of cholesterol a day. The Dietary Guidelines recommend that cholesterol intake be kept below 300 mg a day.

POLYUNSATURATED FATS VERSUS SATURATED FATS—IS BUTTER BETTER?

Another kind of fat, saturated fat, has been associated with heart disease. Increasing the saturated fat intake in one's diet tends to increase the blood cholesterol. Saturated fats—such as butter, fat meat, shortening, lard, and margarine—are generally solid at room temperature. The most highly saturated of the animal fats are lamb, beef and pork fat. Chicken fat is less saturated and it is evident in that it is not as solid at room temperature as so-called "red" meats. Margarine is generally less saturated than butter, but you should read the label to make sure.

Monounsaturated fats, such as olive oil, have no effect on blood cholesterol. Olive oil will neither raise it nor lower it.

Polyunsaturated fats are generally liquid at room temperature and have been shown to have a cholesterol-lowering effect. Increasing PUFAs (polyunsaturated fats) in the diet has been demonstrated to reduce the incidence of heart disease. Most vegetable fats are polyunsaturated with the exception of coconut oil and palm oil.

Many people will substitute whipped topping for whipped cream and coffee whitener for cream in the coffee to reduce fat in the diet. Whipped topping and coffee whitener are made of coconut oil, which is 80 percent saturated, while butterfat in whipped cream or coffee cream is only 40 percent saturated. In this case, cream would be a better choice, for a number of reasons. New technology has made it possible for us to invent foods that never existed before, such as coffee whiteners, whipped toppings, imitation sour cream (also from coconut oil), margarine and a great variety of snack foods and convenience foods. These synthetic foods are low in nutritive value and may actually be harmful.

CIS TO TRANS—AN UNNATURAL ACT

In a study of the effects of altering dietary fat in men at risk for heart disease, an important discovery was made. The men who were put on diets that substituted vegetable oil (high in polyunsaturated fats) for animal fat were found to have a lower incidence of heart disease but a higher incidence of cancer! Laboratory studies showed that PUFAs increased tumor growth more than saturated fats did.

The next question was, "why?". The natural molecular configuration of vegetable oils is for the fatty acid chains to be on the same side of the molecule, and the chemical term for that is "cis configuration." In processing and refining vegetable oils, some of the fatty acid chains are twisted to the other side of the molecule into what is called the "trans configuration."

The trans configuration is not found in our natural food supply, yet consumption of trans fatty acids has tripled in the past 60 years, due to our heavy consumption of processed and synthetic foods. Though the exact mechanism of action is not known, we do know that it is during the processing of the fat that the molecular change occurs. This could happen when oils are hydrogenated to make margarine, shortening or any number of food additives. This change in molecular configuration also occurs when fats are heated to a high temperature over a period of time as happens with deep-fat frying, particularly in fast food restaurants where the fat is used over and over again.

Farmers have known for years that diet can affect the quality of fat in the animal, making it either more or less tender. Corn-fed beef is especially tender because of the effect of the PUFA in the corn on the texture of the meat, perhaps because of an alteration in the cell membrane. This same principle could explain how the trans fatty acids behave in the human body. Changes in the cell membrane could affect cell permeability, allowing more carcinogens to enter, thus increasing the risk of cancer. Another possible explanation is that the changes in fatty acids in the interior of the cell could make it more conducive to tumor growth. Or it might be that high levels of PUFAs could depress the immune system.

Faced with this evidence, it appears that the consumer has a difficult choice. Eat saturated fats and get heart disease or eat polyunsaturated fats and get cancer. The wisest course would probably be to eat less total fat, avoid fried foods, and consider olive oil and butter instead of margarine and other fat choices for the small amount of fat that you do eat.

When there is a great deal of confusion about what to do, as in this case, try to reflect on the natural order of things. Man was probably not meant to eat meat. If you look at carnivorous animals, they have large canine teeth for ripping flesh. We do not. Our teeth are better designed to gnash vegetable food. Our saliva contains ptyalin, an enzyme that breaks down starch in the mouth, which aids in the digestion of food from vegetable sources.

Nature provides an abundance of food that is perfectly suited to our bodies. It goes against the order of things to introduce synthethic foods that are not found in nature. The wisest choice is to stick as close as possible to the food patterns that human beings have thrived on for centuries.

INVISIBLE FAT

It is easy to see the fat on a steak and trim it off. Butter and margarine are obviously fat and one can tell how much is eaten simply by looking at it. All fat is not as easily seen or measured.

Much of our food supply has invisible fat in it—fat we cannot see. For example, a slice of pound cake has nine grams of fat which is about the same as the fat content of two slices of bacon. The fat in bacon can be seen but the fat in the pound cake is invisible.

Many baked goods have invisible fat. Those containing the most fat are cakes, cookies, biscuits, piecrust, and pastries. Low-fat cakes include angel food cake, sponge cake and fruitcake. These would be better choices than a layer cake, both in caloric content and in fat content. Puddings are a better choice than pies because of the high-fat content piecrust contains.

In a piece of pie, the piecrust alone has 100 calories and 10 grams of fat. The fat content of the piecrust in a piece of pie is higher than a whole piece of layer cake which has 7 grams of fat. If you eat pie, you may want to leave part of the crust to save a few calories and cut down on fat.

Of all baked goods, probably the highest in fat is Danish pastry at 15 grams of fat per piece. Croissants, which are becoming increasingly popular as sandwich breads, are a type of Danish pastry and are high in fat.

Invisible fat is also found in processed foods. Look on the label to see which ingredients are listed first. Ingredients must be listed in the order of predominance. For example, the ingredient list for a popular instant flavored coffee beverage reads as follows: sugar, hydrogenated coconut oil, corn syrup solids, instant coffee, etc. This indicates that sugar is the predominant ingredient, followed by hydrogenated coconut oil. It is important to read labels because sugar and/or some form of fat are often the main ingredient in many processed foods.

If you follow the dietary pattern outlined in the Longevity Diet, 15 percent of the 1800 calories on the maintenance diet would come from fat. That would be 30 grams of fat a day. The average American eats 143 grams of fat per day. The U.S. Dietary Guidelines suggest that we should keep our fat intake below 60 grams (based on a 2000 calorie diet), you may want to begin by trying to keep your fat intake between 30 and 60 grams a day, with a gradual decrease to a goal nearer 30 grams.

The following chart lists some foods that are commonly eaten, to give you an idea of fat content.

Fat Content in Grams

1 cup skim milk	trace
1 cup lowfat cottage cheese	1
1 tablespoon whipped topping	1
1 tablespoon sour cream	2
3 ounces fish	4
1 cup yogurt	4
3 ounces chicken breast	5
1 egg	6
3 ounces lean sirloin steak	6
1 cup ice milk	7
2 slices bacon	8
1 tablespoon peanut butter	8
1 cup whole milk	9
1 ounce cheese, (cheddar, Swiss, American)	9
1 cup rich ice cream	24
3 ounces lean and fat sirloin steak	27

FAST FOOD FILLS MORE THAN YOUR STOMACH

Because fast food has become such a dominant part of today's lifestyle, it is important to point out the impact that it has on the American diet. The average American consumes one-third of his meals away from home and fast food makes up a large portion of those meals. Fast foods are generally high in calories, fat, sodium and sugar and are low in fiber.

A typical meal might include a quarter-pound hamburger with cheese, french fries, and a chocolate shake. That meal has 1116 calories and 51 grams fo fat in it! In a single fast-food meal, we can easily exceed both the recommended calorie limit and the fat intake for a whole day. If a person were to eat like that for several weeks, months or years, they would very probably gain weight, and become at risk for developing high blood cholesterol and hardening of the arteries.

The best idea is to keep our intake of fast foods to a minimum but when we must eat fast food, there are choices that could help us keep the fat and calorie level down. A plain hamburger generally has 257 calories and 9 grams of fat. Water is a good beverage and is available at no charge. Tea, coffee and juice have no fat and are also alternatives to shakes. Some fast-food restaurants have salad bars and are adding more healthful items to the menu—such as baked potatoes and broccoli—all the time. If you order a baked potato, ask for the toppings on the side so that you can control how much you put on.

WHAT YOU CAN DO

1. *Move in the direction of a vegetarian diet*, consuming more fruits, vegetables, and grains and less meat.
2. *Eat more fish and white, skinned meat of chicken or turkey.*
3. *Substitute skim milk for whole milk and low-fat cheese for some of the whole milk cheeses.*
4. *Increase consumption of apples and oatmeal.*
5. *Maintain ideal weight.*
6. *Reduce overall fat intake.* Avoid fried foods, trim the fat from meat, skim the fat from gravy, do not add fat to vegetables.
7. *When you use fat, use olive oil or butter.*

8. *When a recipe says to saute vegetables in fat, cook them in a non-stick pan with a little water and no fat.*
9. *Use salad dressing instead of mayonnaise.* (One tablespoon of mayonnaise has 100 calories and 11 grams of fat. One tablespoon of salad dressing has 65 calories and 8 grams of fat.)
10. *Substitute yogurt for sour cream* on baked potatoes and as a topping for other foods where sour cream in normally used.
11. *Try blended cottage cheese as a potato topping* and as a base for dips, in place of sour cream.
12. *Chill gravy and soups and skim the fat off* before reheating them to be served.
13. *Reduce consumption of processed foods.*
14. *When you eat out, try restaurants that offer salads and vegetables.* At fast food restaurants, order the smaller burgers and skip the fries and shakes.
15. *If you must eat away from home often, consider taking nutritious foods with you* instead of eating out all the time.
16. *Avoid pastries.* Low-fat breads are French and Italian bread, bagels, most loaf breads and some cornbread. Avoid croissants and limit biscuits.
17. *For dessert, eat more fruit and low-fat dairy products,* such as yogurt and ice milk. Choose puddings and crustless pies instead of pies with pastry crusts.
18. *Use milk in your coffee (or drink it black) instead of creamers.*
19. *Try wine vinegar as a salad dressing instead of oily dressings*

CHAPTER V

THE CARBOHYDRATE CONNECTION

SENSUAL SWEETNESS

Americans, accustomed to the good life, have acquired a national sweet tooth. The average American consumes about 125 pounds of sugar a year or roughly one cup a day. One-fourth of this sugar is consumed in soft drinks, averaging 36 gallons per person per year. These are average amounts, so while some of us consume less than a cup of sugar a day, others consume much more. Some teenage boys consume as much as 400 pounds of sugar a year, mostly in soft drinks and snack foods.

At the beginning of this century, Americans were getting about 85% of their calories from complex carbohydrates (starchy foods that are high in fiber) such as whole grain breads and cereals, legumes, nuts, potatoes, and other vegetables. Today carbohydrate foods provide only 45–48% of the average American's total caloric intake, but over one-half of this is in the form of sugar and sweets.

Heart disease, diverticulitis, and diabetes occur mostly in developed, affluent countries where individuals eat high-fat, high-sugar diets lower in fiber than any previous national diets in human history. On the other hand, these diseases occur far less frequently in the so-called undeveloped nations where they eat a low-fat, low-sugar, high-fiber diet. This suggests there may be a carbohydrate connection between these diseases and dietary intake.

THE ORIGINS OF A SWEET TOOTH

As man evolved, he had to experiment to find which foods were edible. With some exceptions, it was found that bitter foods often induced illness, while sweet foods rarely produced illness or death. This led to a preference for sweets not only for taste but also for safety.

Our taste buds are trained from an early age to desire sweets. An infant naturally prefers sweet foods and will not accept other foods if sweets are introduced too early. A child whose early diet is high in sugar may gradually want to eat more and more sugar, because too much sugar can actually decrease a person's ability to taste the sweetness of food. At the same time, the ability to taste other flavors is sharply reduced. A person who is exposed early and continuously to sweet tastes may grow to prefer sweetness and reject other flavors.

The sense of taste diminishes with age. Infants have taste buds not only on the tongue, but on the roof of the mouth, the cheeks and even the lips. By early childhood the taste buds are mostly concentrated on the tongue. In adulthood, taste bud loss begins around the age of 40. This is hastened and escalated if the person smokes, doubling the taste bud loss. With decreased taste sensation, older people tend to oversweeten and oversalt foods to get the same taste they remember from earlier times.

THE SUGAR VILLAINS

There have been a number of books written about the evils of sugar and sugar addiction, attributing to it such ills as violent behavior, hyperactivity and even murder. But in fact, there is no scientific evidence to suggest that sugar causes this kind of behavior. Instead, the evidence suggests that there are three main problems caused by overconsumption of sugar.

The first problem with over sugaring is that the sugar may replace healthier foods and interfere with proper nutrition. One can only hold a certain amount of food. If a large portion of that food is concentrated sweets, which offer no nutrients except calories, then there is no room for more nutritious foods and the possibility of malnutrition arises.

The second problem is weight. Even if a person eats a reasonable diet, if they also eat a lot of sweets, then they will in all probability become overweight. With the average American intake of sugar about one cup a day, that adds up to 770 "empty" calories. ("Empty calories" refers to foods that contribute no nutrients except calories.) Sugar is an empty calorie food.

As we age, the basal metabolic rate slows, and we need fewer calories to maintain our body weight. That is why many people, even though they may be consuming the same amount of food they always have, become overweight in their 50's or 60's. This slowing of the metabolic rate is of particular concern when we continue to eat sugary foods. Since we need fewer calories to maintain our weight as we grow older, it is especially important that those calories contribute needed nutrients to our diet. (It is not realistic, however, to expect people to totally eliminate sugar from the diet, since it is one of life's little pleasures.)

The biggest problem with sugar is tooth decay. Dental caries has reached epidemic proportions in this country. Ninety-eight percent of American children have some tooth decay and half of the people age 55 or older have none of their original teeth. Americans spend $10 billion a year for dental care.

Sugar is a favorite food of bacteria. When sugar is present on the teeth, a chain reaction of events quickly begins. Bacteria in the mouth break the sugar down into acids, and the acids dissolve calcium from the tooth enamel. When the protective layer of calcium is gone, tooth decay can grow. Sucrose, the simple carbohydrate in sugar, can be changed to acids more easily than starch, a complex carbohydrate.

The form that the sugar is in and when it is eaten are perhaps even more important than the amount consumed. A sticky caramel that clings to teeth may cause more dental problems than a soft drink. Sweets that are in constant contact with the teeth are the worst villains, such as hard candy, mints, chewing gum and the constant sipping of soft drinks (which results in a constant bathing of the teeth in a sweet fluid). Sugared foods eaten between meals are more likely to cause cavities than the same foods eaten with a meal, because other foods in the meal help to dilute the effect of sugar on the teeth. Even when the food is consumed at the end of the meal there is still a dilution effect because of increased saliva flow from eating.

HONEY—A ROMANTIC SWEET

Perhaps it's something about the flowers and the bees that has caused people to think of honey as a food with special qualities. The fact is, honey is no more nutritious than refined sugar. It is more concentrated, sweeter, and it contains more calories than sugar (honey—65 calories per tablespoon and sugar—51 calories per tablespoon). Honey, like sugar, is an empty-calorie food and there are no scientific studies that suggest that honey has any effect on arthritis or that it has any other curative effects.

OTHER "VIRTUOUS" SWEETS

Some people believe that raw sugar, brown sugar and turbinado sugar are much more nutritious than table sugar. Brown sugar may contain a trace of some minerals, depending on how it was processed, but the amount is negligible, certainly not enough to make a significant contribution to the diet.

Raw sugar is tan or brown in appearance and is a coarse, granulated solid obtained from evaporation of sugarcane juice. FDA regulations prohibit the sale of raw sugar unless impurities—dirt, insect fragments, etc. are removed. Health fadists tout it, but the evidence suggests it is no more nutritious than table sugar.

Turbinado sugar is sometimes viewed erroneously as a raw sugar. Actually, it has to go through a refining process to remove impurities and most of the molasses. It is edible if produced under proper conditions; however, some samples have been found to contain contaminants, according to the Sugar Association. Turbinado sugar is also an empty calorie food and offers no known advantages over other forms of sugar.

ARE CEREALS REALLY CANDY?

Reports on the percentage of sugar in various cereals are impressive, but can also be misleading. While a one-ounce serving of cereal may be 39% sugar (by weight) and have 11 grams of sugar, a 12-ounce soft drink may be only 10% sugar (by weight) but have 37 grams. When selecting cereal, consider the following:

1. Total nutritive value of the product
2. Amount of sugar in the cereal
3. Whether extra sugar will be added at the table
4. Are you being overly concerned about sugar in cereals while your family consumes greater amounts of sugar in other foods?

You may want to select cereals that are lower in sugar. The following list of cereals, all relatively low in sugar, is arranged in order of increasing sugar content from the cereal with the least sugar content to the one with the most: Shredded Wheat, Cheerios, Wheat Chex, Grape Nut Flakes, Puffed Wheat, Post Toasties, Product 19, Corn Total, Special K, Wheaties and Corn Flakes.

Although they have gotten a "healthy" reputation through skillful advertising, granola cereals can be deceiving. Many brands are packed with sugar and fat. One brand of granola is 22% sugar, compared to 1% sugar in shredded wheat. It is easy to consume too many calories when eating granola. One-fourth cup of granola has 130 calories. Most people would not be satisfied with a one-fourth cup serving. One cup of Wheaties has 110 calories by comparison.

Since most cereals have at least a moderately sweet taste, try them without added sugar. Fresh or dried fruits could add sweetness. Eventually you could become accustomed to having your cereal without added sugar. Who ever said that breakfast foods had to be sweet anyway?

THE SUGAR-DIABETES CONNECTION

Wealthier countries consume more sugar and less starch than the underdeveloped countries. Generally, rates of diabetes are low in countries where starch consumption is high. Changing dietary patterns in countries such as Israel, Africa, and Japan, including an increase in sugar consumption, have correlated with an increase in the rate of diabetes mellitus. Although sugar is restricted in diabetic treatment, there is no real evidence that shows a continuous or high consumption of sugar causes diabetes. The cause of diabetes still remains unknown as does the cure.

The factors most strongly associated with diabetes are genetic inheritance and obesity. There are very few cases of diabetes in populations where there is little obesity. When one becomes obese, abnormal glucose (sugar) tolerance may develop and high blood sugar may occur. Fat cells become insulin resistant but this is often reversed by weight loss. Though sugar intake can't be said to cause diabetes, sugar can contribute to obesity which increases a person's risk of getting diabetes.

SUGAR AND MOOD SWINGS

Many things can give us a good feeling—being in love, watching the ocean waves roll in, standing on a mountain top looking at the scenery. But if our blood sugar level is not right, nothing else will be right either. We may be unable to think clearly and may feel weak and shaky. We are more likely to make errors and we may become anxious, easily upset, irritable or depressed. We may develop a headache and feel dizzy and nauseated. These are the signs of hypoglycemia, or too little glucose in the blood. This is a temporary imbalance and many of us have experienced it at one time or another. Hypoglycemia has been reported in one out of every five women under the age of 45.

The health and functioning of every cell in the body depend on blood sugar. The brain depends exclusively upon sugar (glucose) energy and is especially vulnerable to a temporary deficit in the blood sugar supply. When the brain is deprived of energy, mental processes are affected.

Food is usually a quick cure for temporary low blood sugar, but this solution can backfire if the food contains too heavy a concentration of sweets. For example, if you eat a candy bar to relieve the symptoms, you will probably get relief within a few minutes. But the body reacts to high levels of sugar on an empty stomach by oversecreting insulin in a quick attempt to metabolize the sugar. The result is that soon you may feel the same symptoms again.

The best way to handle the symptoms of low blood sugar is to eat a meal or snack that contains some starch, protein and fat. This mix of nutrients will keep the food in the stomach longer and cause the insulin to be released gradually instead of in a big rush. If sweet foods are eaten, it is best to eat them with a meal so that the other foods will dilute the concentrated sugar, preventing you from feeling weak, shaky and irritable later.

Instead of a candy bar as a snack, try nuts, cheese and fruit or milk and crackers. If you must have your daily ration of chocolate, it would be better to have it as dessert with your meal.

BAD PRESS FOR STARCHES

The popularity of the high-protein diet (a dangerous diet not recommended by nutrition professionals) misled the public into thinking that protein was a magical food, while carbohydrates were sinfully fattening and to be avoided. It is not uncommon for someone to go to a restaurant, order an eight-ounce steak and ask the waiter to hold the potato because they are dieting, saving 90 calories while eating a 500 calorie steak. If the dieter ate the potato and only half of the steak, they would be better off.

The American public has always believed starchy foods have little nutritional value and were surprised when the U.S. Dietary Guidelines suggested that we increase the consumption of starchy foods (complex carbohydrates) and "naturally occurring" sugars (mainly those from fruit). Starchy foods include potatoes, breads, cereals, pasta, corn, sweet potatoes, beans, legumes, and rice. The benefits of increasing your intake of complex carbohydrates are:

1. It crowds out meat and fatty foods in the diet.
2. It would increase fiber in the diet.

These recommendations changed our whole approach to meal planning. Today vegetarian meals are considered healthier than meat-centered ones and when meat is eaten, it is considered healthier to eat less of it. It is perfectly acceptable to serve two starchy foods at the same meal, such as beans and corn or potatoes and lima beans. In fact, certain combinations of these complex carbohydrates can yield protein of the same quality as the protein in meat. The next chapter will give you guidelines to follow in planning meals that have complete protein without using meat.

BRANTASTIC BENEFITS

Dietary fiber is the portion of plants which is not broken down by chemical action in the digestive system. Fiber, commonly called roughage a few generations ago, only occurs in plant foods. The meat-centered, high-fat, low-fiber diet of most Americans has been accompanied by a greater incidence of heart disease, colon cancer and diverticular disease than is found in countries where people eat a high-fiber, more vegetarian diet. It is thought that the reduction of fiber content in our national diet over the years may have contributed to the higher incidence of these diseases in the U.S.

Years ago, fiber was thought to be a useless component in foods, since it contributes no real nutritive value. However, we have since learned a great deal about the role of fiber in the diet.

One benefit of fiber in the diet is its laxative effect. Since fiber holds water, stools produced by a high fiber diet tend to be bulkier and softer. They pass more quickly and more easily through the intestines, causing less strain and pressure on the bowel and blood vessels. With more frequent bowel movements, the bowel tissues are less likely to be exposed to toxins and cancer causing substances because of the faster transit time.

Fiber's laxative effect is most pronounced in foods that contain bran, such as bran cereals and whole grain foods. However, too much bran in the diet can cause loose stools, flatulence (intestinal gas), and a feeling of being "stuffed" or "bloated." It can also interfere with mineral absorption. Bran should never be eaten dry because as the body's moisture causes it to expand it can cause choking and/or clog the digestive system.

Fiber in the diet has been shown to diminish the amount of cholesterol the body absorbs from food and may even alter the amount of cholesterol formed in the liver. Increased fiber reduces the transit time of the food through the intestines, leaving less time for cholesterol to be absorbed. This cholesterol-lowering effect was observed with pectin, which is found in apples, peaches, grapes and some other fruits and vegetables.

A high fiber diet may also be helpful in losing weight, since it requires more chewing and tends to satisfy the hunger impulse sooner. In terms of weight loss the high-fiber diet (if not carried to excess) is healthier than a high-protein diet.

The average person today consumes about 4 grams of crude fiber a day, compared to about 6 grams in 1900. It would probably be beneficial to increase that consumption to about 6 grams. A list of foods and their fiber content follows to provide you with some guidelines for planning high-fiber meals:

Food	Serving Size	Crude Fiber in Grams
All Bran Cereal	1/2 cup	3.0
Apple (with skin)	1 medium	2.0

Prunes	1/2 cup	1.5
Dried beans	1/2 cup	1.5
Melon	1/2 cup	1.0
Broccoli, carrots	1/2 cup	1.0
Wheat Bran	1/2 cup	.8
Potato (with skin)	1 medium	.8
Corn, tomatoes, greens	1/2 cup	.7
Whole wheat bread	1 slice	.4
Most cereals	1/2 cup	.3
White bread	1 slice	.1

WHAT YOU CAN DO

1. *Limit your intake of sugar.* Serve fresh fruit for dessert more often. Try strawberries and bananas or a cantaloupe half filled with grapes or berries or simply fresh apples and cheese. As you prepare fruit combinations for salads and desserts, remember that any combination of fruits is delicious and nutritious, so be creative.

2. *Select canned fruits that are water packed* or packed in a light syrup.

3. *Select cereals that are lower in sugar.*

4. *Instead of sugary soft drinks*, try water with lemon in a frosted glass, fruit juice or skim milk.

5. *Choose fruit for a low-calorie snack.* When is the last time you savored the juicy, fresh flavor of an orange, the sweet crunch of an apple or the sensuous sweetness of a ripe melon or peach? If you are watching your weight, fruit is an especially nice snack, since peeling an orange can occupy your hands as well as reaching into a bag of chips while you're watching TV.

The Carbohydrate Connection

6. *Reduce sugar in recipes.* For example, when fixing a baked apple, use one teaspoon of sugar instead of one tablespoon of sugar.

7. *When entertaining, avoid serving a rich dessert.* Many people would actually prefer a simple plate of fruit and cheese.

8. *Eat an apple at coffee break* while everyone else has a sweet pastry or donut.

9. *Don't make all your party refreshments sweet and/or fattening.* Try banana chunks dipped in lemon juice and rolled in finely chopped nuts. Spear on toothpicks. Or dip apple and pear wedges in lemon juice and spread with a cheese spread. Serve fresh vegetables and dip.

10. *Try warm fruit sauces on pancakes* and waffles instead of syrup or honey.

11. *Consume your sweets in liquid form* rather than in a sticky form. For example, a soft drink would not be as bad on your teeth as a caramel candy bar.

12. *Eat sweets with meals rather than during the day.* Each time sugar is eaten, acid that attacks tooth enamel is formed for twenty minutes.

13. *Include some complex carbohydrate, and/or protein* to keep you from having that let-down feeling later from low blood sugar that sweets often give you. Often people feel sick after having eaten pancakes or waffles for breakfast. Syrup is a concentrated sweet and it can cause the insulin to overreact, resulting in low blood sugar later. If you eat a sweet breakfast, include some milk, cheese or egg to minimize the effect of the sweets on blood sugar.

14. *Increase the fiber in your diet* by eating more fruits and vegetables, whole grain breads and cereals and beans and legumes. Leave the peel on fruits and vegetables, when possible.
15. *Select "whole wheat bread" or "whole grain bread"* rather than just "wheat bread."
16. *Serve a vegetarian meal several times a week (or more).*

CHAPTER VI

THE PROTEIN MYSTIQUE

PROTEIN—THE POWER NUTRIENT

Protein is an essential nutrient and, though protein deficiency is rare in this country, it is often seen in other parts of the world. Populations with low protein intakes are shorter in stature, have lower resistance to disease, shorter lifespan, and higher infant mortality rates. Protein is essential for growth and repair of body tissues, a fact well known to most people due to the advertising media.

In fact, advertisers have done such an effective job in promoting high-protein diets and food supplements that the American public eats about twice as much protein every day as it needs. This is an expensive excess, since protein foods are the highest in cost. It can also be expensive in terms of excess calories and fat consumed, since most meat protein sources are rich in both. There is a certain mystique about protein—perhaps because of its reputation for building strong muscles and melting fat—that has led to many misconceptions. Let's take a look at some common beliefs about protein.

BELIEF: Weight lifters and other athletes should eat large amounts of protein to build muscles.

FACT: Athletes only need normal amounts of protein during training, keeping their calorie intake just high enough to maintain their desired weight. Exercising muscles is what builds strength, along with normal nutrition.

BELIEF: Steak and eggs make the best pre-game meal for optimum performance of athletes.

FACT: Though this is a traditional meal recommended by many coaches, research has revealed that it is too high in protein and fat to permit optimum physical performance. The high protein content draws water into the digestive system, depriving the rest of the body of moisture for proper cooling during the game, while the high fat content of the meal can make an athlete feel heavy and slow. A better pre-game meal would be high in complex carbohydrates, with a moderate amount of protein and a small amount of fat.

BELIEF: Carbohydrates are more fattening than protein.

FACT: The popularity of the high-protein reducing diets gave the impression that carbohydrates were more fattening than protein, but they are actually equal in caloric content. If a person eats more protein than is needed for growth and repair, the excess protein will be used for energy or stored as fat just as it is with carbohydrates.

BELIEF: Meat has the highest quality protein of any food.

FACT: Milk and egg protein are higher quality proteins than meat protein.

BELIEF: There are certain essential nutrients that are found only in meat.

FACT: Plant foods can provide all of the essential nutrients, including protein, if they are eaten in the right combination. Vitamin B–12 is the only exception. It occurs only in meats and dairy products. If someone on a vegetarian diet ate dairy products, their B–12 needs would be met without having to eat meat. If they did not consume dairy products, they would be advised to take a Vitamin B–12 supplement.

"LOSE FIFTEEN POUNDS THE FIRST WEEK!"

The books, *Dr. Atkins' Diet Revolution* and *Dr. Stillman's Quick Weight Loss Diet*, both high-protein diets, proved very popular with American consumers. These diets are meat-centered, very high in protein and consequently high in fat. Because the high-protein diet does result in initial, dramatic weight loss (primarily from dehydration and actual muscle loss) dieters who tried them felt encouraged and stayed with the plan. Most of this weight lost was not fat, but water and lean tissue from muscles and organs such as the liver. Muscle was broken down to get the much-needed glucose, fuel for the brain, which high-protein diets lack. Loss of lean body tissue results in a lower basal metabolic rate since lean tissue is more metabolically active than compared, say, to fat tissue. This results in the dieter needing even fewer calories to maintain their weight.

As people continued on high-protein diets, their appetite decreased because eating nothing but meat, butter and other rich foods becomes repugnant to the palate after a while. This decrease of appetite caused further reduction in caloric intake which the body perceived as starvation, decreasing the basal metabolic rate (burning fewer calories) as a survival tactic. As a result, the dieter was really burning up fewer calories they were eating on this diet than they would have on a more sensible, satisfying diet that contained more calories. Lack of energy, dizziness, headaches, irritability, and even depression also accompanied this lowering of the basal metabolic rate. At this point, the dieter usually abandoned the diet and quickly regained all of the weight they had lost.

High-protein diets are not recommended for the following reasons:

1. They are too high in fat and dangerously high in cholesterol.

2. They could be particularly dangerous for a person who is prone to kidney disease. When protein is used for energy, there is a great deal of urea produced, which must be handled by the kidneys. High protein diets put a heavy work load on the kidneys. That is why promoters recommend that you drink a lot of water while on these diets.

3. They could be dangerous for diabetics because they are already at risk for heart disease and large amounts of fat in the diet could mean trouble.

4. Most of the weight loss is lean body tissue and water and the weight is quickly regained when the diet is abandoned.

5. They do not promote healthful lifetime eating habits.

6. They are low in fiber and could cause constipation.

7. Low caloric intake could cause the basal metabolic rate to drop, making you burn fewer calories.

8. The large amount of urea produced on a high protein diet could make a person prone to gout.

COULD TOO MUCH PROTEIN BE DANGEROUS?

Several studies have been done to determine the effects of high protein diets. It is known that infants and children do not thrive on diets containing large amounts of protein. Animals fed large amounts of protein develop enlarged livers and kidneys. There appears to be no advantages in a diet that is more than 15 percent protein, more protein than that crowds out other needed nutrients.

COMPLETE PROTEIN WITHOUT MEAT

Long-lived peoples eat mostly vegetarian diets and benefit from the advantages of eating less meat. Many Americans are concerned about shifting to a more vegetarian diet and wonder if they can get all of the nutrients they need from one. However, clinical tests have shown that even children thrive on vegetarian diets (provided that the right combinations of vegetables are eaten). Vegetarian meals may require more planning to ensure the presence of complete protein, but they are worth the trouble.

GETTING THE ESSENTIALS

There are eight essential amino acids and they must all be eaten at the same time and in the correct proportions in order for us to get complete proteins. (Complete proteins contain all of the eight essential amino acids). Animal foods, such as eggs, milk, fish and meat are complete proteins because they have the right amount of all eight amino acids. Most plant foods are incomplete proteins in that they are missing one or more amino acids.

Those eating a vegetarian diet can easily get high quality, complete protein by combining the right plant foods. For example, corn is an incomplete protein, but when it is eaten with beans, another incomplete protein, the beans provide the amino acids that the corn doesn't have, and vice versa. However, the two foods must be eaten at the same meal to get complementary proteins. This would not work, if you had the corn for lunch and the beans for dinner.

Though this method of menu planning may seem quite different at first, it is interesting to discover how many of these combinations we are already eating in our normal diet. For example, many people regularly eat pinto beans and cornbread. No meat is needed at a meal like this because the combination of plant foods gives the same complete protein that meat has.

Below is a list of food combinations that make complete protein and some examples of menu items to be served.

Beans and corn

Use any kind of dried beans and serve with any style of corn or corn product.

Dried beans and cornbread

Bean enchiladas or bean tacos

A vegetable plate that includes dried beans and corn

Check cookbooks for further ideas. Many Mexican recipes offer interesting possibilities based on this combination. Beans can also be substituted for ground beef in many recipes.

Beans and rice

Black beans and rice is a popular dish with a Spanish flavor that uses this combination and there are many recipes for it. Look in Mexican cookbooks and also for New Orleans-style recipes.

Another dish that includes this combination is a traditional Southern food that is served on New Year's Day, Hopping John, which is seasoned dried black-eyed peas served over rice.

Milk and wheat

    Cereal and milk

    Bread and cheese (cheese sandwich)

    Macaroni and cheese (or any other wheat pasta product with milk and/or cheese, such as manicotti)

Peanuts plus wheat, oats, corn, rice or coconut

    Peanut butter sandwich (wheat in bread)

    Stir-fried vegetables over rice with peanuts (check Chinese recipes or make up your own)

    Trail mix, party mix or granola mixture that includes peanuts with prepared cereals made from wheat, oats, corn and/or rice

Soy protein plus corn, wheat, or sesame

    See this section on tofu for ideas

Legumes plus cereals

    Beans and wheat—use wheat bulgur instead of rice, or dried beans with wheat bread

Leafy vegetables plus cereals

    Serve wheat bread, rice or bulgar with meals that contain leafy vegetables or prepare casseroles that combine these foods.

Milk with beans, peanuts, rice or legumes

Since milk is already a complete protein, it completes the amino acid deficit in any food. Serve milk, cheese or yogurt with meals to get complete protein from plant foods.

There are several excellent recipe books containing delicious and imaginative vegetarian dishes. Here are a few: *Diet For a Small Planet*, by Frances Moore Lappe, *Recipes For a Small Planet*, by Ellen Buchman Ewald, *Laurel's Kitchen*, by Robertson, Flinders and Godfrey, and *The Vegetarian Epicure*, by Anna Thomas. The first two books use some unfamiliar ingredients, such as miso, brewer's yeast, and soy flour. If you are a beginner and these seen too advanced, the last two books use more familiar ingredients.

TOFU

Tofu, (also known as soybean curd), is a versatile food made from soybeans. Although unfamiliar to many, tofu is worth looking into because it is a valuable, low-cost source of protein. It is sold in 16-ounce cakes that are water-packed and packaged in plastic tubs or cartons and can be found in the refrigerated section of the grocery store, usually with the produce. Tofu is ivory in color and about the texture of cheesecake. It is also mild in flavor and it takes on the taste of whatever ingredients it is combined with. Tofu is so versatile that you could enjoy tofu enchiladas for the main dish and end the meal with a fruit-topped tofu cheesecake.

There are many advantages to using tofu. It is inexpensive, low in calories (about 70 calories per three-ounce serving), low in fat and high in protein and calcium. The calcium content is of particular importance because few foods other than dairy products have so much calcium in them. Soybean products have been used for years in baby formulas because they are so nutritious. Equal weights of tofu and whole milk are nearly equal in caloric content, protein content, and calcium content. This makes tofu an important food since it can be substituted for meat and yields even greater nutritional benefits because it is lower in calories and fat than meat, yet provides valuable protein. Additionally, meat is not a significant source of calcium and tofu is.

Since tofu is low in cost and can be made to taste just about any way you want, it is worth some experimentation to find ways you or your family like it. Be sure not to judge it based on how tofu tastes out of the package because it doesn't taste like anything. You add the flavor. You can make tofu "meat balls" for spaghetti or patties or desserts. There are some recipes using tofu in the books listed above. You also may want to get the recipe book, *The Book of Tofu—Food for Mankind*, by William Shurtleff and Akiko Aoyagi.

GELATIN, THE PROTEIN WEAKLING

Gelatin has been advertised for years as a protein supplement that helps build strong nails and hair. Actually it is an incomplete form of protein and contributes nothing to the growth of strong nails or hair. A better protein for growing strong nails and hair would be complete protein chosen from the correct combinations of vegetable proteins or milk, egg, meat or fish protein. In fact, if gelatin is used as a protein supplement, it can actually reduce the benefit of the other proteins in one's diet by flooding the system with extra amino acids that have to be disposed of, crowding out some of the amino acids the body actually needs.

WHAT YOU CAN DO

1. *Eat less meat* and serve more vegetarian meals. If your family enjoys a meat-centered diet, begin with a meatless meal once a week and increase the frequency as they begin to accept them.
2. *Try vegetarian recipes* and consider their potential for variety. There are basically only five different kinds of meat and poultry but there are 40–50 different kinds of commonly eaten vegetables and 20 different kinds of fruits, 24 kinds of beans, peas and lentils, 12 different kinds of nuts and nine kinds of grains to choose from. Combinations of these foods could offer practically limitless variety.
3. *Experiment with tofu* to build a file of favorite family recipes.
4. *Avoid high protein diets* and concentrate on a healthier diet that is high in complex carbohydrates (fruits, vegetables and grains).

CHAPTER VII

PREVENTING BONE LOSS AND OSTEOPOROSIS

"SHE FELL AND BROKE HER HIP"

There seems to be an epidemic of hip fractures in older people. We often hear that someone (often a woman) just retired, planning to travel and pursue new hobbies and interests and then they fell and broke their hip.

Osteoporosis, a disorder that results in bone loss, making the bones brittle and prone to fracture, strikes one in four postmenopausal women. The bones become so fragile that simple movements, such as turning at the sink to put away a dish, or simply walking, could cause a fracture. In all likelihood, the bone may have broken before the individual fell, so we might be more accurate to say: "She broke her hip and it made her fall."

Osteoporosis is more prevalent in women than in men, but both sexes have a higher incidence of fractures with advancing age. Ninety percent of all bone fractures past the age of 60 are thought to be caused by osteoporosis. Over one billion dollars a year are spent in the care of patients with hip fractures, and that does not include the human cost in suffering, physical disability, and mortality associated with this disease.

Current research has begun to discover some possible causes of bone loss, giving clues to its prevention. Diet, physical activity and hormonal factors are all thought to be strongly assocciated with the development of osteoporosis at this point.

BUILDING STRONG BONES

In pregnancy and early life, attention should be focused on building bones that are as strong as possible. In later life, we need to focus on minimizing the age-related bone loss that is apparently inevitable. Peak skeletal mass is attained around the age of thirty and is greatly influenced by dietary intake of calcium. Bone loss begins around the age of forty, but for women, following menopause, it accelerates to two or three times that of men.

Men have greater bone density than women throughout life and that may be why they have a lower incidence of osteoporosis than women—they have more bone to lose. Women may have less bone because they exercise less or because they consume less calcium in their diet. Often women will stop drinking milk to save calories and start drinking soft drinks, which interfere with calcium absorption. Repeated pregnancies also may result in increased bone loss.

Since bone loss accelerates with menopause or hysterectomy, it is thought that it may be influenced by hormones. Some physicians prescribe estrogen for postmenopausal women who are at risk for osteoporosis, but there are hazards involved. Estrogen therapy has been associated with increased risk of uterine and breast cancers. Fortunately, there are other options. Increasing one's calcium intake is a safer alternative to estrogen therapy and has been shown to effectively reduce bone loss in many cases.

The average intake of calcium in postmenopausal women is 600 milligrams (mg) per day or less. It is recommended that they increase the daily intake to 1500 mg/day. Younger women need less, about 1000 mg/day. Most dietary sources of calcium are generally adequate, so supplements are usually not necessary unless a person cannot consume dairy products. An 8-ounce glass of skim milk or its equivalent in yogurt or cheese contains about 300 mg of calcium. Tofu, sardines, canned salmon, oysters, collard greens, spinach, mustard greens, and dried beans are also good sources. Dairy products and tofu or soy products are by far the richest sources of calcium, however.

CALCIUM INTAKE AND FRACTURE RISK

Several studies have indicated that a diet that is high in calcium actually reduces the incidence of fractures among senior citizens. This evidence is strong enough to encourage people of all ages to be sure they get an adequate amount of calcium in their diet if they wish to minimize the risk of broken bones.

DIETARY INTERACTIONS

There are several factors in the diet that can interfere with calcium absorption, such as alcohol, caffeine, protein and phosphorous. People who consume large amounts of alcohol over time are more likely to have reduced bone mass and a higher incidence of fractures. High caffeine intake also causes bone loss. One cup of coffee contains enough caffeine to cause 6 mg/day of calcium to be lost. This suggests that high caffeine intake should be avoided and if you do consume caffeine, you will need extra calcium to make up for the loss.

High protein intake interferes with calcium absorption, another reason to avoid high protein diets. Phosphorus, an essential mineral, is usually present in foods that are high in protein, such as meat. Calcium and phosphorus compete for absorption and when there is much more phosphorus present than calcium, it decreases calcium absorption. Many popular foods are high in phosphorus: meat, processed foods and soft drinks. For optimum absorption of calcium, the calcium to phosphorus ratio in our diets should be 1:1, which is found in dairy products. In contrast, in a pork chop the ratio is 1:22 and in liver 1:44, telling evidence of just how a meat-centered diet can crowd out needed calcium.

PHYSICAL ACTIVITY AND LIFESTYLE

Dramatic bone loss often occurs in weightless space and during longterm bedrest. Since people tend to be less active as they grow older, this evidence suggests that decreased physical activity may be a factor in age-related bone loss.

We know that mechanical stress on the body is necessary for building bone density. Mechanical stress is what occurs when your foot hits the pavement when you walk or run. It is also present when you hit the ball with the racket during a tennis match. In a study of tennis players, it was found that the players' tennis arms had denser bone than their other arms.

Walking, running and weight lifting are excellent exercises for increasing bone density. Cycling is fair but swimming, an excellent aerobic exercise, does not produce mechanical stress. This makes it a good exercise for people with disabilities but an ineffective one for increasing bone density.

Healthy persons should exercise as regularly and as vigorously as possible to maintain bone density. Individuals with fractures or disabilities should do their best to sustain an exercise program adapted for their particular disability, in order to prevent bone loss from inactivity. As discussed in Chapter II, even people at advanced ages can begin an exercise program and reap its benefits.

One lifestyle factor strongly associated with bone loss is cigarette smoking. Cigarette smoking is associated with a higher incidence of osteoporosis and more fractures, probably due to some chemical interaction as yet unknown.

WHAT YOU CAN DO

1. *Women should increase their intake of calcium to 1000 mg/day* before menopause and 1500 mg/day after menopause. Men should consume about 1000 mg/day of calcium in adulthood.
2. *Begin a regular exercise program* that you enjoy and can continue as an on-going part of your lifestyle.
3. *Be careful not to overconsume meat* and phosphorus-containing foods, such as processed foods and soft drinks.
4. *Reduce consumption of soft drinks* and drink more water, juice and milk.

5. *Do not smoke.*

6. *Calcium should be consumed daily* because the body has a limited ability to absorb calcium. You cannot eat massive doses of calcium today and skip it tomorrow and expect to have optimum absorption.

7. *Limit fat in the diet* because high-fat consumption inhibits calcium absorption.

8. *Be sure you have some milk* and a little sunshine everyday because Vitamin D, which is in milk and also in sunshine, enhances the body's capacity to absorb calcium. (Vitamin D is not actually present in sunshine but when the ultraviolet rays it contains reach our skin, Vitamin D is produced in the cells.)

CHAPTER VIII

TOWARD LIFETIME WEIGHT CONTROL

FAT BABY, FAT FOREVER?

Only a few years ago, mothers bragged about how fat their babies were and competed to see whose baby ate the most and started on solid food first. Now we know that fat babies are not healthy babies and fatness in infancy lays the groundwork for chronic weight problems because the fat cells an individual will possess for a lifetime are developed during the first year of life.

If the individual was fat as a baby, then they developed more fat cells than normal and will always have the same number of fat cells no matter how much they may reduce their food intake later in life. When such people attempt to lose weight by dieting their cells merely shrink in size, requiring only a slight change in dietary habits (a small eating binge, for instance) to regain their original mass. It is important that mothers be conscious of this and not overfeed their babies. Obesity that began in early life is the most difficult to treat. If a child is overweight and has not reached normal weight by the time they are twelve years old, they have only a one-in-four chance of ever becoming a normal weight adult. If they are still overweight at the age of 18, they only have one chance in twenty-eight of ever maintaining a normal weight for their age group.

Obesity that begins in adulthood (adult onset obesity) is much easier to treat. In this case the fat cells that were developed in infancy expand, but more fat cells are not produced. Adult onset obesity is a direct result of an individual's maintaining their childhood eating habits after adulthood has slowed their metabolic rate.

THE REAL COST OF OBESITY

Although most people think obesity results from an excess of nutrition, obesity is, in fact, a form of malnutrition, the most widespread form. It has been associated with increased incidence of diabetes, hypertension, hyperlipidemia, gout, arteriosclerosis, arthritis, hernia, and gallbladder disease. The incidence of hypertension can be up to three to five times higher in individuals who are 50% or more above optimum weight. Obese individuals also run a higher risk of some forms of cancer and more problems with joint diseases. An obese person has an average life expectancy 13 years shorter than that of an individual of normal weight.

Obesity is reversible, however: Mortality rates are no higher for the formerly obese than for those who were never obese. Losing weight usually results in lower blood pressure, lower blood cholesterol and blood glucose levels, and reduced uric acid concentrations (associated with gout). These positive changes reduce the risks of heart disease and diabetes. A major study reported that if everyone were at optimum weight, there would be 25 percent less heart disease and 35 percent fewer strokes.

Obesity causes internal changes as well as changes in outward appearance. One study reported obese men in their thirties as having psycho-physiological profiles very similar to those of 71-year-old men. With the reduced life expectancy (13–15 years) of overweight people, obesity could be regarded as a form of premature aging.

Being overweight can also be a social and economic disadvantage. Overweight individuals are less sought after for marriage, less likely to get into the college of their choice, and are often discriminated against when applying for jobs and promotions. In 1978 it was reported that as a result of this discrimination an obese male could lose $279,050 in lifetime earnings (compared to normal weight males), while the cost of food for maintaining 100 pounds of extra weight could add an average of $500 or more per year to the grocery bill. Americans spend another half a billion dollars annually on diet books, reducing aids, and unnecessary diet supplements.

WHY WE OVEREAT

When a baby cries, the mother sticks a bottle in their mouth. When a child falls down, the mother gives them a cookie to soothe their feelings. When someone dies, friends bring food to comfort the family. We learn at an early age that food provides immediate gratification and makes us feel better.

Soon we begin to associate feeling down with a need to eat more. This can become a vicious cycle: Overeating makes us feel guilty, then we need food to make us feel better, which only makes us feel guilty again. This pattern, begun in childhood, can be broken if we take the time to learn other ways to cope with negative moods and deal with the stresses of everyday life.

Have you ever felt you wanted something to eat, but you didn't know what it was? You peer into the refrigerator and sample some cheese and maybe a piece of pie. When that doesn't satisfy your craving, you rummage through the cabinets, looking for whatever it is you want but can't define. The truth is you are not really hungry, you are bored. Because your environment is unstimulating, your unconscious prompts you to search out pleasurable sensation from food. The activity occupies your time for a little while and the food tastes good.

Eating for pleasure instead of to satisfy hunger could be called recreational eating. Some writers call it grazing. Whatever you call it, it is a costly way to spend your time, in terms of calories and money. Next time you get that vague craving, take a good look at your life and try to think of ways to make it more interesting so that you won't need to eat to relieve boredom. Chapter ten will have suggestions for pleasant things to do for yourself that will make you feel as good or better than eating for fun.

Sometimes people overeat to get back at those they love. For example, a daughter may overeat to declare her independence from an overprotective or nagging mother. Or a wife may overeat to get back at her husband for any number of reasons. This may not necessarily be conscious, since overeating has the worst consequences for the person doing the overeating.

If you have reason to think you are a compulsive eater, you need to get in touch with your real feelings and find out why. Sometimes it helps to talk the situation out with someone, or write down your feelings in a journal.

Some people say they overeat simply because they enjoy the taste of food. It is so pleasurable that they cannot stop. If people truly enjoy food, they would savor it, tasting every mouthful.

It is an established fact that 99.5% of all overweight people are fast eaters. Eating food more slowly results in a more satisfied feeling and consequently in eating less. It takes twenty minutes for the stomach to signal to the brain that it is getting enough food to be satisfied. A fast eater can cram down a lot of food in twenty minutes, resulting in a painful, bloated feeling.

You should make an effort to take at least twenty minutes to eat every meal and ten minutes for every snack. Time yourself. It may be a little difficult at first, but chew your food well and take the time to taste the subtleties of flavor. Put down your fork between bites. Talk to your family. Or daydream. But take twenty minutes.

If I had to name one thing that determines the success in a weight reduction plan, it would be self monitoring. Each day write down everything you eat, including snacks, meals and little tastes here and there. This serves several purposes: it makes you aware of what you are eating, it helps you identify problem times of day and situations, and knowing that you will have a record of it makes you think twice before eating something. The day someone stops writing this list is usually the day they abandon their weight control program.

Plan what you will eat in advance—think before you eat. Planning takes pressure off you when you are hungry and weak. You will already have made a decision about what you will be eating. This is particularly important during holidays when you go to parties and are faced with many temptations. Be sure to save calories and plan for some little indulgences. But if you do get out of control, don't worry about it, just go right back to your normal program. Don't try to starve the next day to make up for mistakes.

HOW TO STOP RECREATIONAL EATING

There is a great deal of evidence to suggest that overweight people do not experience hunger the same way that normal weight people do. An experiment was done in which subjects swallowed a balloon that could measure stomach contractions. They were told to record every time they felt a stomach contraction (or hunger pang). Normal weight people reported hunger pangs each time the stomach contracted. The overweight subjects never felt hungry even during the stomach contractions. This suggests that eating is not internally stimulated in the obese but is caused by outside influences or external cues.

Research tends to show that things in the environment have more of an influence on the eating behavior of overweight people than do internal body signals. Seeing, smelling, and talking about food are the factors that cause overweight people to feel hungry and eat. External cues—such as the smell of a bakery, the sight of candy in a candy dish or watching a television commercial for food—can all stimulate eating behavior in overweight people. That is why overweight people will eat meals at mealtime, whether they are hungry or not (the external cue of time is enough to influence them).

A number of experiments have illustrated the importance of external cues in the eating behavior of overweight individuals. In one when subjects were hungry they were given a nutritionally balanced, bland liquid from a feeding machine designed to conceal the food so that the subjects could not see how much they were eating. The subjects were told to eat whenever they felt hungry and to eat as much as they wanted. The normal weight subjects ate just enough of the food to maintain their weight, indicating they responded to internal hunger symptoms. The overweight subjects ate much less, indicating the influences of external cues on their eating behavior: Since they could not see or smell the food, they were not inclined to eat much of it.

Because external cues can influence their eating behavior, it is important to keep food out of sight to prevent overeating. Put desserts in the back of the refrigerator and in the back of the cabinets. Put the candy dish and the cookie jar away. Don't use see-through cake stands.

Psychologists have developed several behavior modification techniques that help change habits for lifetime weight control:

1. Make eating a pure experience. Don't do other things while you eat, such as read the paper, work around the house, watch TV, talk on the phone, or ride in the car. When you eat, just eat and enjoy the food and the company you are in.
2. Choose a specific place in one room of your home to do all of your eating. This will be your designated appropriate eating place. All meals and snacks should be eaten there, and only there. (Of course, you could have a different place for each meal.)
3. Remove food from all places in the house except appropriate storage areas such as the kitchen. Keep food in opaque containers that you cannot see through.
4. Have raw vegetables prepared for eating in the refrigerator so that you can substitute them for junk food when you get the urge to nibble.
5. Do not take seconds on servings and do not keep serving containers on the table while you eat. If this is not

possible, put the serving dishes at the other end of the table from where you sit.

6. Take at least 20 minutes to eat a meal and 10 minutes to eat a snack. Time yourself.

7. Put your fork or spoon down between each bite, to slow your eating speed.

8. Set aside a time each day to think ahead and to plan your food intake. Include all food and drink for the day that has significant caloric value.

9. Write down what you will eat for each meal and snack. Count the calories to be sure you have 1200. Budget calories where necessary.

10. Use different colored pens to check off the things you ate and record any additions or corrections. As you become better at pre-planning, the number of two-colored entries will decrease.

11. Plan ahead for eating out and for parties. How many drinks will I have? How can I budget to keep from eating too much?

12. Pre-plan what you will buy. Junk food not bought is junk food not eaten. Go to the store on a full stomach and stick to the list.

13. Never eat standing up. This will eliminate tasting in the kitchen, eating in the refrigerator, snacks at cocktail parties, and many other tempting situations.

14. Never accept food from another person unless you asked for it. This helps you stick to your pre-planned list.

15. Throw away leftover food or save it for another meal. Do not clean up other people's plates by eating the leftovers.

16. Think of activities you could do that are incompatible with eating—things that it would be difficult to do while eating, such as taking a shower, playing the piano, doing needlework, singing. Next time you get the urge to eat, do one of these things instead.
17. Think to the immediate future—how will I feel five minutes from now after the small pleasure of eating this is past? (guilty, fat, sorry).

IMAGERY AND VISUALIZATION FOR A THINNER YOU

Some behaviorists have suggested aversion techniques for weight control, such as taping pictures of fat people on the refrigerator door, thinking of bugs in your food, and imagining that the food will make you sick. These techniques do not work successfully for most people.

Better results have been obtained when subjects use imagery and visualization to plant a positive image in their mind. Here are the steps:

1. Find a quiet place where you can sit comfortably in a chair and relax without being disturbed. (Be careful not to get so relaxed that you go to sleep.)
2. Close your eyes and relax all of the muscles in your body by first contracting (or squeezing) them and then relaxing them. Begin with your neck. Roll your neck three times to the right, then three times to the left. Now relax your shoulders. Shrug them—hold the position for a minute, relax. Next push down on the armrest of the chair as hard as you can—hold the position for a few seconds, let go. Then make a fist, hold it, then relax. Suck in your stomach, hold it, relax.

Squeeze your buttocks, hold them, then relax. Press your feet hard against the floor, then relax. You'll be amazed at how relaxed you've become, how much tension you've released. Mentally survey your body to be sure that all of your muscles are completely relaxed.

4. Think of the most beautiful, peaceful place you have ever been. It may have been the mountains, the desert, the beach or the country. Imagine yourself in that place right now. What does it look like? What colors and textures do you see? What are the scents like there? Do you smell salt air, a pine forest or a field of flowers? What are the sounds? Do you hear the wind, the waves, the birds singing? Do you feel the sun on your back, the wind or the crisp fall air, or snow? Try to visualize and sense every detail of your mental landscape so that it really feels like you are there.

5. Now think of yourself as you would like to be—thin, healthy and in control of your life. How does that make you feel? Imagine every detail of it. Do you walk differently, think about yourself differently, relate to others differently, does your body feel healthier? From this moment on, pretend that you have already achieved your goals. Pretend that you are now thin, healthy and in control of your life. Take those feelings with you always and let every aspect of your behavior reflect the new you. You can approach food differently now. Think of it as a healthy, pleasurable part of your life, one that helps you meet the goal of looking and feeling your best. When you feel hungry between meals, think of this in a positive light, as a sign that you are on your way to the goal of becoming thinner. Instead of being a chore, exercise can

now become a pleasurable experience, one that allows you to feel your body move and perform for you at your command. You feel yourself becoming stronger and shapelier every day. Enjoy the rush of air into your lungs as you exert yourself, feel the sweat produced by doing something nice for yourself that could also be the start of a lifetime of healthier habits and being.

6. Remember these feelings and take the thoughts with you everywhere. You are already the person you want to be! So now how will you relate to the world? Put a positive reminder on the refrigerator door that says "thin" or "beautiful" or "healthy forever," or whatever else makes you feel good.

7. When you look into the mirror, see yourself becoming thinner every day. Remember, you are already there, so behave accordingly. Think of yourself in positive terms. Tell yourself that you are thin and looking good and feeling good.

8. Start now to do interesting things that you can do in the place of the eating from boredom that you were doing before (the list in Chapter X will help you get started thinking in that direction).

TRAIN YOUR BODY TO BURN MORE CALORIES

An individual's activity level plays an important role in weight control and in the maintenance of general health. There is considerable research suggesting that people who have weight problems tend to be about half as active as those who do not have weight problems. One study of obese housewives revealed that they spend more of their time in light activities such as sitting, sleeping, and watching television than a similar group of women who were thin.

The average American's calorie intake has decreased since 1900, though the incidence of obesity and overweight individuals has increased. Changes in lifestyle, such as the replacement of walking with the automobile, numerous labor-saving devices for work and home, and the proliferation of sedentary leisure-time activities—such as spectator sports and television viewing—have greatly reduced the expenditure of physical energy by many people.

Since research has shown that most obese individuals do not eat appreciably more than their normal-weight counterparts, an attempt to reduce by severely restricting one's caloric intake through dieting could result in an inadequate supply of essential nutrients. A more effective approach would be some form of increased physical activity along with a reasonable reduced-calorie diet. In the long run this is the only logical way to facilitate weight loss.

Most overweight people fail to realize how much exercise it really takes to produce any significant weight loss. In one study, a group of obese women were asked to estimate the amount of exercise required to consume the caloric value of foods such as doughnuts, ice cream, and potato chips. These women underestimated the true amount of work required by 200 to 300 percent. (Perhaps this is a reflection of the American culture with its emphasis on personal convenience which expects a large return for even moderate exertion.)

Running is an excellent aerobic exercise that promotes cardiovascular fitness and facilitates weight control. Running exercises most of the larger muscles. It expends more energy than pushups or driving a golf ball.

The number of calories expended in running (approximately 100 calories per mile) seems small when compared to the 3500 calories that must be burned to lose over one pound of fat. If running one short mile a day were made a part of your lifestyle, however, you could lose ten pounds a year without changing your food intake at all.

The hypothalamus gland, located at the base of the brain, regulates appetite. It seems to work optimally only when the body gets adequate exercise. In an active person, appetite causes just enough food intake to maintain body weight, but in an inactive person, the hypothalamus does not work effectively and the individual tends to overeat. As a result, regular exercise can actually help a person to desire less food.

By the age of 30, a person's basic energy needs are 10% less than they were at age fifteen. After 30, our calorie needs decline 7% each decade. These decreased energy requirements can produce weight gain even when someone reduces the caloric intake. That is why daily exercise in addition to reducing your caloric consumption is necessary to prevent weight gains or promote weight loss.

The basal metabolic rate remains increased for several hours after exercise, so exercise not only burns calories during activity, but afterward as well. You can actually train your body to burn more calories by engaging in regular physical activity for 20–50 minutes a day several times a week.

There is also reason to believe that the timing of meals may also have an effect on whether or not that food is converted to fat. Food eaten earlier in the day or before physical activity is not as likely to be stored as fat as food that is eaten late in the day or during prolonged periods of inactivity. Exercising a couple of hours after eating tends to burn calories more than if the exercise is done before eating the meal. In this case the old cliche of "walking off the meal" actually seems to have some merit.

The spacing of meals is also important in weight loss. The body stores less fat if our food intake is spread out over the day, in several small meals and snacks, than if food of equal caloric value was eaten at one or two big meals.

FITNESS FOR LIFE

There are many ways to lose weight: diets, drugs, hypnosis, surgery, medication, shots, psychotherapy, etc. All of these may be effective initially, but they usually fail in the long run. The reason for failure is that they do not result in the kind of long term changes in lifestyle which are necessary to produce sustained weight loss. For long term success, it is necessary to learn new habits that can be continued throughout life. You must always be on the look out for ways to cut calories and increase activity.

If you can add only 30 minutes a day of moderate exercise to your schedule you can lose 25 pounds in one year without having to change your eating habits. To put it another way, eating just one extra slice of bread a day or drinking one extra soft drink (or any other food item that contains about 100 calories) can add up to 10 extra pounds to your weight a year. This adds up to a 50-pound weight gain in five years. Yet this weight gain could be prevented by adding a brisk 25 minute walk to your daily schedule.

Most people do not get enough exercise during their ordinary daily routine. Modern technology—from food processors to power steering—made life easier and much less demanding physically. Yet human bodies were designed for activity. For those who have become used to an inactive or sedentary lifestyle getting on a program of regular physical activity requires a definite plan—and a real concerted effort to follow that plan.

Those who wish to increase their level of physical activity have four main approaches to chose from.

1. A regular exercise schedule
2. Recreational activities to supplement daily exercise routines
3. Increased ordinary physical activity
4. Physical activity in the day's occupation

An exercise program should be balanced just as a diet should be balanced. It should include activities that exercise the heart and lungs (aerobic activities), such as running, cycling, swimming, brisk walking or heavy gardening. For optimum results you should engage in some aerobic activity 30 minutes a day five times a week. Other parts of your program should include activities and exercise aimed at increasing strength, flexibility, balance and muscle tone. There are specific exercises for these purposes, and they are included in most calisthenics, aerobic dancing, weight lifting, and a number of others. You might want to buy a record or a videotape to help get you started on a program. Many people enjoy the group approach found in exercise classes and spas. Or you may want to consider investing in a home gym or weight machine.

Your scheduled exercise should be supplemented with additional physical activity. Gardening on weekends, a family outing or fishing trip, bowling or an evening of social or square dancing would provide both fun and exercise. It is important to choose something that you enjoy and will look forward to. Involving friends and family can add to your pleasure.

You can also add a little more activity to your day by walking to the store or a neighbor's house instead of driving. Think of how many times you have circled a parking lot, looking for a space close to the door to save yourself a few extra steps. You could park at the other end of the lot and add the extra walk to your activities. Try taking the stairs instead of the elevator. Stand up to put on your shoes and socks instead of sitting down (this also helps improve the balance). Get up to change the TV channel instead of using the remote control.

And remember, the amount of daily activity in your job is also important. Look for ways of increasing activity on the job—stand up to talk on the phone, walk to deliver a message instead of sending a memo, walk to the files instead of sending someone else, and use your lunch hour for exercise instead of time to consume extra calories.

ENVIRONMENTAL SUPPORT—FAMILY AND FRIENDS

Research shows that those who were most successful at losing weight had the complete support of their spouses and/or friends. You can get this support by telling them what you need. Here are a few suggestions:

1. Ask for what you want—praise, feedback, cooperation, rewards.
2. Get their help practicing the techniques in this book. If you practice together, you will do better.
3. Request friends and acquaintances to not use food as gifts for you. For Valentine's Day, birthdays and other

special occasions, ask that they give you flowers, a favorite recreational activity, or some other gift.

4. Request those in your environment not to offer you food at any time. Let them know that if you want food, you will ask for it. Being offered food is a strong social cue and is difficult to refuse.

5. Try to avoid conversational topics that center on food (this, too, is an external cue that could trigger eating). Let family and friends know that you would rather talk about other things while you are trying to lose weight.

6. Try to entertain without using high calorie foods. Instead of potato chips, offer low-calorie snacks. Your guests will probably appreciate it. When you are visiting someone else, let them know beforehand that you will not be eating as many high calorie foods so they won't be insulted when you turn such foods down.

7. Ask your family not to eat snacks in front of you because that is a strong cue that can stimulate your own urge to eat.

8. Develop exercise programs with other people. Being with others makes exercise more fun, and the social commitment reinforces your resolve to carry the program through.

WHAT YOU CAN DO

1. *Start a notebook in which you will plan what you eat and record everything you eat*, so that you can monitor your progress.

2. *Start a daily checklist for yourself* with the following goals to work toward. Give yourself a checkmark for

each task that is accomplished:
   Planned what I would eat.
   Ate only planned meals and snacks.
   Measured food before eating it.
   Counted calories.
   Exercised.
   Visualized myself as already being thin and healthy.
Put this list in your notebook and check it every day.

3. *Find someone to join you* in your daily exercise program. Start today.
4. *Think of ways that you can add more physical activity* to your daily routine.
5. *Start a new recreational activity*—dancing, gardening, bowling, rowing, etc.—with someone you like.
6. *Think of ways you can add more interest to your life to help eliminate the boredom* that causes you to overeat. Is boring television a cause of your recreational eating? If it is, can you think of more productive ways to use your time?
7. *Buy a calorie counter and for a week or two count the calories* you consume every day. Think of things you would not miss out of your diet that would save you calories. It is very important to be aware of the caloric content in foods so you can make better food choices. For example, some people "skip lunch" and grab a coke, not realizing that they could have had a very satisfying and much more nutritious lunch for the same number of calories they spent on an empty-calorie snack.
8. *Continually think of ways that you can cut fat in recipes* and in the food choices you make. Try shake-

and-bake fish instead of fried fish—it tastes as good as fried and contains fewer calories. Use plain yogurt instead of sour cream on baked potatoes and give up that extra pat of butter. Leave the piecrust on the plate and try ice milk instead of the richest ice cream you can buy. Be creative looking for ways to cut fat—it need not decrease your eating pleasure and it can save more calories than anything else you can do.

CHAPTER IX

THE LONGEVITY DIET

Thin people live longer than overweight people and experimental animals who were fed modest amounts lived almost twice as long as those given a normal diet. The world's long-lived peoples also consume about half as many calories a day (1200–1800) as are found in the average American diet (3000–4000 a day). Furthermore, recent medical research suggests a diet that is low in calories and fat and high in plant foods and fiber can be very beneficial in preventing cancer. Foods high in carotene and Vitamin A and those in the cruciferous family (such as cabbage, broccoli, brussels sprouts and cauliflower) are particularly recommended. Statistics on heart disease yield similar results, suggesting that the vegetarian, low-fat diet also significantly reduces risk of heart attack and stroke.

Many researchers say that it is too early to make recommendations based on these findings, that more research is needed. More research is indeed needed, but in the meantime, in order to be able to make intelligent food choices, based on what is already known, the public has a right to know in which direction these findings are pointing. I call the nutrition program these findings suggest the "Longevity Diet."

It may be difficult to change directly to this kind of diet if you come from a family of heavy meat-eaters or one that always enjoyed fried foods and ones seasoned with meat grease. If you cannot follow all of the suggestions in this chapter at the beginning, try to start with the ones you find easiest to make. You will still be increasing your chances of living a longer and healthier life.

It takes 3500 calories to make a pound of fat (the average adult woman burns around 2000 calories a day, the average man around 2600). To lose a pound of fat in a week, you need to consume 3500 fewer calories than you burn (or about 1250 calories a day). But be sensible and avoid radical diets. Safe weight loss is slow but it is far more likely you will maintain the new weight if you lose it slowly, at the rate of one or two pounds a week (or maybe even less, depending on your age, activity level and present weight), than on a binge or purge. If you do not wish to lose weight, add 500–700 calories a day, following the guidelines given earlier for healthy food choices.

The Longevity Diet emphasizes plant foods, but it is not totally vegetarian. Based on the research findings for prevention of osteoporosis, it includes more calcium than most diets. It also offers great variety and flexibility making it easy to adapt as a lifetime plan.

It would be unrealistic to expect anyone to strictly follow any diet for a lifetime, and when following this diet, it is all right to occasionally binge on a rich dissert, a fried seafood platter or a Danish pastry. What is important for good health and prolonged lifespan is that you adopt the Longevity Diet as your basic food pattern and indulge in "sinful" goodies only on occasion. In addition, you may discover that you enjoy them more when you are eating them less often.

After you have been on this lower-fat program for a while, you may find that you will not be able to eat high-fat foods without some discomfort (feeling bloated) because your body will have adapted to the new, healthier diet. This is a real advantage, because then you will find that you don't even desire these foods anymore.

THE LONGEVITY DIET

CALCIUM GROUP: Select 3 servings per day if you are under 55; 4 servings per day if you are over 55. Selections from this group average about 100 calories each, except for those designated *, which are about 200 each.

Amount	Food
1 c.	Skim milk or nonfat milk
1 c.	Buttermilk
1 c.	Yogurt, plain
4 oz.	Tofu
1 oz.	Cheese, cheddar, American or other
1/2 c.	Cottage cheese
1 c.	Flavored yogurt*
1 c.	Ice milk*
3/4 c.	Baked custard*

*Choose no more than three desserts per week.

PROTEIN GROUP: Choose 2 servings per day. These selections average about 200 calories each, except for the egg (which is only 90 calories). If you select only plant foods (a good idea) remember the combinations for complete protein (Chapter VII). If you are getting your daily complete protein requirements from vegetable combinations (for example, if you have macaroni and cheese and dried beans and cornbread in one day), then your protein needs are already filled and you do not need to select two additional servings from this group.

Amount	Food
1 c.	Dried beans, peas, or lentils
1/2 c.	Baked beans, no pork, canned
3 oz.	Lean beef
3 oz.	Lean pork
3 oz.	Chicken or turkey
2 Tbsp.	Peanut butter
1/4 c.	Peanuts
1/4 c.	Almonds
1°4 c.	Cashew nuts
1 c.	Oysters
3 oz.	Fish
3 oz.	Shrimp
6 oz.	Clams
1 c.	Crabmeat
4 oz.	Salmon
4 oz.	Tuna, packed in water
6 oz.	Sardines, drained
1 c.	Lobster
1	Egg
3 oz.	Tofu

VEGETABLE GROUP: Select at least two servings from this group (more, if you desire). Each serving is approximately 25 calories. Remember, do not season vegetables with fat, particularly meat grease. If you must use fat, use olive oil or butter (but use no more than 1 teaspoon in total per day).

Be sure to get at least one serving of broccoli, cabbage, cauliflower, or brussels sprouts every day. Also, be sure to get at least one serving of a dark green leafy vegetable or a deep yellow vegetable every day (carrots, sweet potatoes, etc.).

Amount	Food
1/2 c.	Asparagus
1/2 c.	Bean sprouts
1/2 c.	Beets
1/2 c.	Broccoli
1/2 c.	Brussels sprouts
1/2 c.	Cabbage
1/2 c.	Carrots
1/2 c.	Cauliflower
1/2 c.	Celery
1/2 c.	Cucumbers
1/2 c.	Eggplant
1/2 c.	Green pepper
1/2 c.	Greens, any kind
1/2 c.	Okra
1/2 c.	Onions
1/2 c.	Rhubarb
1/2 c.	Rutabaga
1/2 c.	String beans, green or yellow
1/2 c.	Summer squash
1/2 c.	Tomatoes
1/2 c.	Tomato juice
1/2 c.	Turnips
1/2 c.	Vegetable juice cocktail
1/2 c.	Zucchini

FRUIT GROUP: You need two servings from this group each day, averaging 40 calories per serving. Be sure that at least one of these servings is a food high in Vitamin C, such as oranges, grapefruit (or their juice), strawberries or papaya. If you would like larger servings of some of the juices, such as grape juice, double the serving size and count it as two servings from this group.

Amount	Food
1	Apple (medium)
1/3 c.	Apple juice
1/2 c.	Applesauce (unsweetened)
2 medium	Apricots, fresh
4 halves	Apricots, dried
1/2 small	Banana
1/2 c.	Blackberries
1/2 c.	Blueberries
1/4 small	Cantalope
10 large	Cherries
1/3 c	Cider
2	Dates
1	Fresh fig
1	Fig, dried
1/2	Grapefruit
1/2 c.	Grapefruit juice
12	Grapes
1/4 c.	Grape juice
1/8	Honeydew melon
1/2 small	Mango
1 small	Nectarine
1	Orange
1/2 c.	Orange juice
3/4 c.	Papaya

1	Peach
1	Pear
1/2 c.	Pineapple
1/3 c.	Pineapple juice
2	Plums
2	Prunes
1/4 c.	Prune juice
1/2 c.	Raspberries
2 Tbsp.	Raisins
3/4 c.	Strawberries
1	Tangerine
1 c.	Watermelon

COMPLEX CARBOHYDRATE GROUP: Select four servings from this group every day. Each serving has about 70 calories each.

Amount	Food
1 slice	Whole wheat (or whole grain) bread
1 6-in.	Tortilla
1 half	English muffin (whole wheat)
1	Corn muffin
1 slice	Cornbread
1	Pancake (5-in, whole wheat)
3/4 c.	Ready-to-eat cereal, unsweetened
1/2 c.	Cereal, cooked
1/2 c.	Grits, cooked
1/2 c.	Rice or barley, cooked
1/2 c.	Pasta, cooked (spaghetti, noodles)
2 c.	Popcorn, popped, no butter
1/4 c.	Wheat germ
5	Crackers (any kind)
1/3 c.	Corn

1	Corn on the cob
1/2 c.	Lima beans
2/3 c.	Parsnips
1/2 c.	Peas, any kind
1	Potato
3/4 c.	Pumpkin
1/2 c.	Squash, winter (acorn or butternut)
1/4 c.	Sweet potato

You may eat unlimited quantities of the following foods:

Garlic, parsley, lemon, lime, chicory, chinese cabbage, lettuce, radishes, watercress, endive, escarole, bamboo shoots, and snow peas.

A QUICK GUIDE TO THE LONGEVITY DIET

Here is a summary of the nutrients and recommended servings from each of the different food groups we have discussed.

CALCIUM GROUP—3 servings per day, 4 servings if you are over the age of 55.

Main nutrients are calcium, protein, riboflavin, thiamin.

PROTEIN GROUP—2 servings unless you have complementary proteins from plant sources. In that case, you may skip servings from this group.

Main nutrients are protein, iron, riboflavin, niacin, thiamin.

VEGETABLE GROUP—2 or more servings a day.

Main nutrients are Vitamin A, Vitamin C, thiamin, additional iron and riboflavin, folacin. This group also contributes fiber.

FRUIT GROUP—2 servings a day.

Vitamins A and C. This group also contributes fiber.

COMPLEX CARBOHYDRATE GROUP—4 servings a day.

Main nutrients are riboflavin, niacin, iron and thiamin. Whole grains are rich in fiber.

HOW TO PRESERVE NUTRIENTS IN FOODS

Many people believe that fresh foods are more nutritious than canned or frozen foods, but that may not always be the case, depending on how the fresh foods were treated. For optimum flavor and nutritional value, vegetables should be prepared for eating as soon as they are gathered. In commercial food canning and freezing, the vegetables are processed immediately to preserve the quality of the food, losing very few nutrients. If fresh foods have sat on the grocery counter (or in your refrigerator) for several days, they may not be as nutritious as those that are canned or frozen.

You can taste the freshness in foods by comparing the sweet taste of fresh corn from the garden with the starchy taste of corn that has been in the refrigerator for three or four days. This corn is probably just as nutritious as the fresh corn, but it doesn't taste as sweet because enzymatic action has converted the sugar to starch, giving the kernels a starchy taste. Summer squash provides another example. Squash also has a very mild but distinct flavor when it is fresh from the garden. After squash has been stored for a few days, its distinctive taste has disappeared. The squash is still good to eat, but has lost its optimum flavor.

The best way to be assured of freshness is to have a home garden and gather the food just before you prepare it. You may be surprised at how naturally sweet vegetables (such as broccoli, asparagus, peas and green beans) taste when they come straight from the garden. With home gardening, you can also control the amount of pesticides and fertilizers you use to ensure the food's safety. There are, of course, other advantages of home gardening: exercise, the stress reduction associated with interaction with living things and the feeling of accomplishment you have when you sit down to a home-grown meal.

Here is a list of techniques for preserving nutrients when preparing food for consumption:

1. Steam or bake vegetables instead of boiling them.
2. When you do boil vegetables use as little water as possible because the water-soluble vitamins dissolve in the water.
3. Leave vegetables in pieces as large as possible when boiling or frying them, to reduce exposure of surface areas to heat and liquid that destroy vitamins they contain.
4. Leave the skin on potatoes and apples, to preserve nutrients and add fiber.
5. Wash apples with soapy water (dish detergent is fine) to remove the waxy pesticides that are on them.
6. Do not soak fruits or vegetables in water because that soaks the vitamins out.
7. Serve Vitamin C foods raw, for optimum nutritive value because Vitamin C is particularly heat sensitive.
8. Do not expose milk to light because riboflavin is light sensitive and could be destroyed. That is why milk is no longer sold in see-through bottles.

9. Save the juices from cooking vegetables to make a delicious and nutritious soup. Put the juices and the leftover vegetables in a big container in the freezer—add to it each day and soon you will have enough for a big pot of the best soup you ever tasted (at no cost).
10. Do not add soda to dried beans. It destroys the nutrients.

THE SODIUM STORY

Sodium plays a major role in maintaining blood volume and pressure by attracting and holding water in the blood vessels. As valuable as sodium is, however, your body needs very little.

High sodium intake is one of several factors believed to contribute to high blood pressure. Some people, particularly those with a family history of high blood pressure, are more apt to develop this condition. It is difficult to know, however, before a problem develops who might benefit from consuming less sodium. It is estimated by the National Institute of Health that about 60 million Americans have some degree of high blood pressure. Untreated high blood pressure can lead to heart attack, stroke, and kidney disease.

One teaspoon of salt contains about 2000 mg of sodium. The National Research Council suggests that a "safe and adequate" sodium intake per day is about 1100 to 3300 mg for an adult. The average adult consumes between 2300 and 6900 mg a day.

Some estimates suggest that as much as one-third of the average daily intake of sodium comes from salt added to food in cooking or at the table. How much salt do you add?

Try this test: Cover a plate with wax paper or foil. Salt the plate as you would if it contained food. Collect the salt and measure it. If you used about 1/8 teaspoon, that amounts to 250 mg of sodium.

Other sources of high sodium are processed foods, canned foods such as pork and beans, and canned soups. Soy sauce has more sodium (1000 mg per tablespoon) than any other condiment that is commonly used in U.S. kitchens. Cured meats such as ham, bacon, bologna and cold cuts are also high in sodium as are pickles and salty snacks, such as potato chips and salted nuts.

You can reduce sodium in your diet in the following ways:

1. Do not salt food before tasting it.
2. If you use salt, use it only once. For example, if the food was cooked with salt added, there is no need to add more salt at the table.
3. Shake the salt shaker only half as many times as usual.
4. Try lemon juice, vinegar and herbs and spices for added flavor instead of so much salt.
5. Try unsalted nuts or nuts that have reduced sodium.
6. Limit the salty snacks you choose. Consider fresh fruit instead.
7. Balance your sodium intake as you do your calories. If you have a high sodium breakfast, have a low-sodium dinner.
8. Limit your intake of processed foods. This is a useful recommendation for many reasons.

WHAT YOU CAN DO

1. *Study this diet* and try as many of the recommendations as you think your family will accept.
2. *If you need to consume more than 1250 calories a day, choose fruits, whole grains, yogurt or snacks and desserts that incorporate these foods for additional calories.*
3. *Experiment with foods and recipes that are lower in sodium.*
4. *Think of food as a pleasure to grow, prepare and eat.* Let it make you healthy and strong, as it was designed to do.

CHAPTER X

LIFE ENRICHMENT AND LONGEVITY

Surprisingly, there is more to living a long and happy life than good genes, healthy food and exercise. Because we are human, we aspire to be more than blind procreators of our species, as the animals are. Our intelligence has given us not only the ability to meet our basic needs for survival, but the desire for higher attainments, such as love, new experiences, creation of new ideas and solutions to problems. Humans are by nature gregarious animals and we need contact with other humans to flourish psychologically and creatively. (That is why solitary confinement is such harsh punishment.) We need challenges and involvement to keep us alert and interested in the world around us. This chapter will suggest ways to prolong your life by enriching it.

HOW TO GET WHAT YOU WANT

Before you can get what you want, you need to know what you want. This involves a complete life assessment to see what your long-term goals are and where you are in attaining them. Goal setting is simple, but it requires some uninterrupted time for creative thought and introspection. Allow yourself a block of three hours to think and plan. Find a comfortable, quiet place and get a tablet and a pen. It's helpful to divide goals into twelve categories:

1. Career or job position
2. Salary or earnings
3. Personal relationships
4. Family relationships
5. Health and weight
6. Travel
7. Financial assets or material possessions
8. Education, specific skills or knowledge
9. Free time or play
10. Home or apartment
11. Transportation
12. Spirituality

List your ideal goals under each category for the next year, then the next six months, then the next three months. After you are satisfied that these goals really reflect what you want, copy them on 3 × 5–inch cards and keep those cards with your "To Do" list. Review those cards every day before you prepare your "To Do" list to be sure that you are doing something that day to bring you closer to your goals. It's easy to get caught up in the minutia of our daily routines and days, weeks and years can go by without our really accomplishing those things we want most. Learn to stay on top of your goals and make good things happen for yourself.

LEAVE YOUR COMFORT ZONE

Comfort zones are those places where you feel most comfortable and in control of the situation, such as your home, your office, your car. These are places we go to think, work and relax and we expect things to be fairly predictable in them, that's why they are our comfort zones. We are also in our comfort zones around certain people, such as family and close friends.

To achieve personal growth, we must leave those comfort zones and venture into new territory, meet new people, try new things. This involves change and challenge, which many of us resist at first. One study has suggested that we need to leave our comfort zone seven times a day for sustained personal growth. When is the last time you left your comfort zone? Meet new people, go to a new restaurant, visit a place you've never been, try a new skill, learn a foreign language, take a chance.

GET RID OF ENERGY VAMPIRES

Even if you are well nourished and well exercised, you still may feel drained of energy at times. Negative people are the worst energy drains of all because they take away your enthusiasm, shoot down your ideas, chip away at your self confidence and leave you feeling weak and drained. When that happens, look at what is happening in your life and identify it. Surround yourself with successful people who live healthy lifestyles, expect success and get it.

Worry and guilt are useless emotions that consume too much energy and produce nothing beneficial in return. Feeling guilty does no one any good. Worry is the fear that something bad might happen and 98% of the time, it never does. Even when something bad does happen, worrying about it beforehand never helps the situation. Instead of wasting energy on worry or guilt, try concentrating on positive things so that you can move forward and grow.

Procrastination is a paralyzing energy drain and it fills you with dread over what you haven't done. When this happens, look at your goals and see how important the thing is you have been putting off. If it is important, DO IT NOW! That's all there is to it. Not later, not tomorrow, DO IT NOW! Think of the feeling of relief and accomplishment you will have when the dreaded task is done. Ask yourself, "What is the best use of my time right now?" Remember that, as Benjamin Franklin said, "Time is the stuff that life is made of."

Sometimes our energy becomes drained simply because we have allowed ourselves to become overcommitted. When this happens, try to figure out ways to simplify your life—cancel activities, delegate tasks, say "No." Hire or ask for help.

Be on the lookout for people and situations that steal your energy and take an active stance against them. Get ready to say "No" and enjoy doing it.

WAYS TO BE NICE TO YOURSELF

Mood is directly affected by things that happen in your environment. For example, if several positive things happen to you, you are more likely to be in a positive mood (and vice versa). Since we are in control of many things that happen in the environment, there are always some nice things you can do for yourself to ensure you'll be in a good mood most of the time. Surround yourself with the things, colors, music and people you love at home and whenever possible at work.

Following is a list of some simple pleasures that you may want to enjoy more often. Write down how many times you have done any of these in the past week. You may want to add other things you enjoy to this list.

Celebration of Self

1. Take time to enjoy nature
2. Take private time for yourself
3. Have a luxurious bath
4. Enjoy a massage
5. Play with an animal
6. Buy yourself a gift
7. Smell flowers and/or other pleasant scents
8. Go on a trip especially for your pleasure
9. Have an evening out for your pleasure
10. Read for pleasure
11. Listen to music
12. Play a musical instrument
13. Dance
14. Sing
15. Tend a garden or plants
16. Pursue a hobby that you enjoy
17. Enjoy a special meal
18. Laugh
19. Dress up
20. Sex play

Health and Fitness

1. Participate in some kind of exercise
2. Eat nutritious food
3. Drink adequate water
4. Get enough sleep
5. Meditation and/or prayer
6. Go for a long walk
7. Enjoy stillness, relaxing alone
8. Wear seat belts in the car
9. Avoid smoking
10. Avoid overeating

Personal Growth—New Experiences

1. Learn something new
2. Develop a new skill
3. Meet new people
4. Try something new
5. Explore an interesting place
6. Go to a concert, play or opera
7. Read a good novel
8. Spend quality time with people you like
9. Take a chance
10. Give of yourself to others
11. Pursue a cause outside of yourself
12. Watch good TV programs

Time Management

1. Determine lifetime goals
2. Pursue lifetime goals
3. Set priorities
4. Begin an important task
5. Complete an important task
6. Write a "Do List" and do it
7. Plan your day
8. Eliminate non-essentials and clutter from your day
9. Review your day. Reflect on accomplishments

Self-Talk

1. Say nice things to yourself about yourself. "I am attractive, lovable, worthy, smart, special, good at . . . , etc."
2. Review letters of commendation, awards, recognition, etc.
3. Write down your thoughts, feelings and creative ideas
4. Project yourself as the person you want to become

THE IMPORTANCE OF TOUCH

As we age, our eyesight may become less effective, our hearing become less acute, our taste buds fewer in number and our sense of small diminished, but the sense of touch remains a source of pleasure and comfort even into advanced age. Touching is more critical to human well-being than one might imagine. Infants who have all of their physical needs satisfied but who are not held, cuddled and touched, will die.

In one university study rabbits were fed a high-fat diet to induce arteriosclerosis. The study showed that the rabbits who were on the high-fat diet but were picked up, held and petted by the students had only half as much fat deposit build-up in the blood vessels as the rabbits who were not held and touched. Cuddling and touching *apparently lowered blood pressure and blood lipid formation.*

Hugging can lift depression and strengthen the immune system, though the mechanism involved is not yet known. It can also strengthen relationships and add pleasure to your day. Research has shown that hugging increases the amount of hemoglobin in the blood, which carries oxygen to all parts of the body, keeping the energy level up. Touching and caressing can reduce blood pressure, having a calming effect. Some physicians prescribe four to six hugs a day. That would seem to be a safe minimum dosage for all healthy people (and it might help prevent more expensive medical treatment later on).

Unfortunately, Americans are not a touching society. We are conditioned by our culture to distance ourselves from each other, resulting in a lot of lonely, affection-starved people. We hold and touch baby girls more often than baby boys and we discourage displays of affection between the same sex and even between opposite sexes if the two are not married or otherwise attached to each other. Americans tend to associate touch only with a prelude to sex, resulting in a loss of many worthwhile tactile pleasures in life. This situation is especially unfortunate for those who are not married, since they can become starved for human contact. Many widows have stated sadly that it has been years since anyone has hugged or touched them. One elderly lady in a nursing home said that she wished she had been more tactile with her children when they were young because now when they visit her, they may bring gifts and offer casual conversation, but never a hug or any touching, which she needs far more.

A study done in Europe compared the amount of touching between American and French dating couples during lunch. The American couples, it was found, touched an average of four times during lunch, while the French couples touched over 100 times! Another study investigated the effect of touch on the attitude of library patrons toward the library. As people checked out the books, the librarian casually touched their hands as she handed them the books. It was found that those who were touched had a more positive feeling toward the library than those who were not, though they often could not explain exactly why. Most of them did not even remember that they had been touched, but evidently the act had some kind of effect on their subconscious mind.

Human contact brings us closer together. It makes us feel better about ourselves and about the world in general. Perhaps we would all be a little stronger, happier and healthier with more touching in our lives. If you are not a tactile person, you may need to begin touching others gradually, but try.

WHAT YOU CAN DO

1. *Determine your lifetime goals* and do something each day that will bring you closer to them.
2. *Leave your comfort zone at least seven times a day.*
3. *Be nice to yourself*, beginning with the methods listed in this chapter, then developing others of your own.
4. *Hug the ones you love*, hold their hands, pat them on the back. Let touching add some warmth and caring to your life.

5. *Identify and get rid of energy vampires.*
6. *Share the things you learned from this book with someone you love.*

May you live a long and healthy life, filled with love and wonder.

BIBLIOGRAPHY

Akroyd & Doughty. *Legumes in Human Nutrition.* Rome, Italy: United Nations, 1964.

Albanese, Anthony. *Nutrition for the Elderly.* New York: Alan R. Liss, Inc., 1980.

Allsen & Harrison, Vance. *Fitness for Life.* Dubuque, Iowa: W. C. Brown, 1984.

Bayrd & Quilter, *Food For Champions. How to Eat to Win.* Boston: Houghton Mifflin, 1982.

Berland, R. *Rating the Diets.* New York: Rand McNally & Co., 1974.

Bray, G.A. *Obesity in America.* Washington, D.C.: U.S. Government Printing, 1980.

Chandra & Newberne. *Nutrition, Immunity and Infection.* New York: Plenum Press, 1977.

Clydesdale & Francis. *Food, Nutrition and You.* Englewood Cliffs, NJ: Prentice-Hall, 1977.

Deutsch, Ronald M. *The New Nuts Among the Berries.* Palo Alto, CA: Bull, 1977.

Feldman, L.P. *Consumer Protection.* St. Paul: West, 1980.

Ferguson, James. *Learning to Eat.* Palo Alto, CA: Bull, 1975.

Food Advisory Board, *A Profile of Older Americans.* Rye, New York: ITT Continental Baking Co., 1981.

Gansong. *Review of Medical Physiology.* Los Angeles: Lange Medical Pub., 1979.

Hafen, Brent. *Overweight & Obesity: Causes, Fallacies, Treatment.* Provo, Utah: Brigham Young University, 1975.

Hafen, Brent Q. *Nutrition, Food and Weight Control.* Boston: Allyn & Bacon, 1981.

Hill & Stone. *Success Through a Positive Mental Attitude.* New York: Pocket Books, 1977.

Jokyl, E. *Nutrition, Exercise, and Body Composition.* Springfield, Illinois: Charles C. Thomas, 1964.

Kart & Metress. *Aging and Health: Biologic and Social Perspectives.* London: Addison-Wesley, 1978.

Katch & Ardle. *Nutrition, Weight Control and Exercise.* Philadelphia: Lea & Febiger, 1983.

Lappe, Frances M. *Diet for a Small Planet.* New York: Ballantine, 1971.

Nash & Long. *Taking Charge of Your Weight and Well-Being.* Palo Alto, CA. Bull, 1978.

National Research Co. *Assessing Changing Food Consumption Patterns.* Washington, D.C.: National Academy Press, 1981.

National Research Co., *Diet, Nutrition, and Cancer.* Washington, D.C.: National Academy Press, 1982.

Natow & Heslin. *Geriatric Nutrition.* Boston: CBI Publishing Co., 1980.

Netter, F. *Fad Diets Can Be Deadly*, Hicksville, N.Y.: Exposition Press, 1975.

Parizkova, Jana. *Nutrition, Physical Fitness, and Health.* Baltimore: University Park Press, 1978.

Parkinson & Brown. *Annual Review of Nutrition.* Los Angeles: Annual Reviews, Inc., 1981.

Roe, Daphne. *Geriatric Nutrition.* Englewood Cliffs, NJ: Prentice-Hall, Inc., 1983.

Rosenberger, J. *The Methuselah Factors*. New York: Pinnacle Books, 1984.

Shuman & Others. *Source Book on Foods and Nutrition*. Chicago, 1980.

Shurtleff & Aoyagi. *The Book of Tofu, Food for Mankind*. New York: Ballantine, 1975.

Sipple & McNutt. *Sugars in Nutrition*. New York: Academic, 1974.

Smith, Nathan. *Food for Sport*. Palo Alto, CA: Bull, 1976.

Stuart & Davis. *Slim Chance in a Fat World*. Champaign, Illinois: Research Press Co., 1972.

Stull, G. Alan. *Encyclopedia of Physical Education, Fitness, and Sports*. Salt Lake City, Utah: Brighton, 1980.

Tyndall, E.A. *A Comparison of Two Nutrition Education Programs for Weight Control*. Ann Arbor, Michigan: University Microfilms, 1983.

Whitney & Hamilton. *Understanding Nutrition*. New York: West, 1981.

Wilson & Brownell. *Advances in Behaviour Research and Therapy*. New York: Pergamon, 1980.

Young, D. R. *Physical Performance, Fitness and Diet*. Springfield, Illinois: Charles C. Thomas, 1977.

Periodicals

"Calcium in Bone Health." *Dairy Council Digest*, 1976,47(6), pp. 31–36.

"Dietary Fiber." *Contemporary Nutrition*, Sept., 1979.

"Effect of Obesity and Weight Reduction on Body Composition." *Nutrition Reviews*, 1962,20, pp.348–350.

"Guidelines for a National Nutrition Policy." *Nutrition Reviews*, 1980,38(2), pp. 96–98.

"Malnutrition Among the Elderly." *Nutrition and Food Science*, 1980, 65, pp. 6–9.

"Symposium: Nutrition in the Causation of Cancer." *Cancer Research*, 1975,35(2).

"Treating Obesity: Three Approaches." *Medical World News*, Aug., 1971, pp. 20–36.

Abramson & Stinson. "Boredom and Eating in Obese and Non-Obese Individuals." *Addictive Behaviors*, 1977 2(4), pp. 181–185.

Albanese, A. A. "Calcium Nutrition in the Elderly." *Postgraduate Medicine*, 1978, 63, pp. 167–172.

Albanese, A.A. "Nutritional Aspects of Bone Loss." *Food & Nutrition News*, 1975,47(1), pp. 1–4.

Alcantara & Speckman. "Diet, Nutrition and Cancer." *American Journal of Clinical Nutrition*, 1976,29, pp. 1035–1046.

Anderson & Chen. "Plant Fiber: Carbohydrate and Lipid Metabolism." *American Journal of Clinical Nutrition*, 1979, 32, pp. 346–363.

Anholm, A. C. "The Relationship of a Vegetarian Diet to Blood Pressure." *Preventive Medicine*, 1978,7(1), p.35.

Avioli, L.V. "Postmenopausal Osteoporosis: Prevention Versus Cure." *Federation Proceedings*, 1981, 40, pp. 2418–2422.

Bazarre, I. L. "Aging and Nutrition Education." *Educational Gerontology*, 1978, 3, pp. 149–163.

Bergan & Brown. "Nutritional Status of "New" Vegetarians." *American Dietetic Assoc. Journal*, 1980,76(2), pp. 151–155.

Burkitt, D. "Epidemiology of Cancer of the Colon and Rectum." *Cancer*, 1971, 28, pp. 3–13.

Carroll & Modan. "Role of Diet in Cancer Etiology." *Cancer*, 1977,40, pp.1887–1891.

Carter, L. J., "How to Assess Cancer Risks." *Science*, 1979,204, pp.811–816.

Chalmers, T. C. "Effects of Ascorbic Acid on the Common

Cold." *American Journal of Medicine*, 1975, 58, pp.532–536.

Cohen, B. L. "Relative Risk of Saccharin and Calorie Ingestion." *Science*, 1978, 199, p. 93.

Dawber & Others. "Coronary Heart Disease in the Framingham Study." *American Journal of Public Health*, Apr., 1957, pp.4–23.

Draper & Scythes. "Calcium, Phosphorous, and Osteoporosis." *Federation Proceedings*, 1981, 40, pp. 2434–2438.

Dwyer, Johanna. "Vegetarianism." *Contemporary Nutrition*, June, 1979.

Ederer, F. "Cancer Among Men on Cholesterol-Lowering Diets." *Lancet*, 1971,2, pp.203–206.

Eisdorfer, C. "Some Variables Relating to Longevity in Humans." *Epidemiology of Aging*, 1982, pp.77–711.

Gilmore, R. L. "Recognizing Problems of the Aging Spine." *Geriatrics*, 1980,35(11, pp. 83–92.

Gordon & Vaughan. "The Role of Estrogens in Osteoporosis." *Geriatrics*, 1977,32(9), pp. 42–48.

Greene, J. "Nutritional Care Consideration of Older Americans." *Journal of the National Medical Assoc.*, 1979,71(8), pp.791–793.

Grupta, C. P. "Nutrition in Geriatrics." *Journal of the Indian Medical Assoc.*, 1980, 74, pp.91–93.

Haenszel & Others. "Mortality From Cancer Among Japanese in the U.S." *Journal of the National Cancer Instit.*, 1968, 40, pp.43–67.

Harger, B. S. "The Caloric Cost of Running." *Journal of the American Medical Assoc.*, 1974, 228, pp.482–483.

Harper, A. E. "Recommended Dietary Allowances for the Elderly." *Geriatrics*, 1978, 33, pp.73–80.

Harris, M. B. "Self-Directed Program for Weight Control." *Journal of Abnormal Psychology*, 1969,74(2), pp.263–270.

Hopkins, H. "Controlling Diet Food Claims." *FDA Consumer*, Oct., 1977, p.16.

Jokyl, E. "Physical Activity and Body Composition: Fitness and Fatness." *Annals of the N.Y. Academy of Science*, 1963, 110, pp.778-794.

Jowsey, J. "Osteoporosis: Dealing With a Crippling Bone Disease." *Geriatrics*, 1977,32(7), pp. 41-50.

Jowsey, J. "Why is Mineral Nutrition Important in Osteoporosis?" *Geriatrics*, 1978,33(8), pp.39-48.

Kannel & Others. "Cholesterol in the Prediction of Atherosclerotic Disease." *Annals of Internal Medicine*, 1979, 90, pp.85-91.

Khari & Johnston. "What We Know—and Don't Know About Bone Loss in the Elderly." *Geriatrics*, 1978,33(11, pp.67-76.

Levitz, L. S. "Behavior Therapy in Treating Obesity." *Journal Of The American Dietetic Assoc.*, 1973, 62, pp. 22-26.

Linkswiler & Zemel. "Calcium to Phosphorous Ratios." *Contemporary Nutrition*, May, 1979.

Majonnier, L. "The National Diet-Heart Study: Assessment of Dietary Adherence" *Journal of the American Dietetics Assoc.*, 1968, 52, pp.288-292.

Marx, J. L. "Osteoporosis: New Help for Thinning Bones." *Science*, 1980, 207, pp.628-630.

Meyer, B. "Exercise and the Cardiovascular System." *Physician and Sports Medicine*, 1979,7(22), pp.54-71.

Morris, J.N. "Vigorous Exercise in Leisure-Time: Protection Against Coronary Heart Disease." *Lancet*, 1977, 2, pp.1207-1210.

Orkow & Ross. "Weight Reduction Through Nutrition Education and Counseling." *Journal of Nutrition Education*, 1975, 7(2), pp.65-67.

Panenbaum & Others. "Policy Statement: Saccharin." *Diabetes Care*, 1979, 72, p. 59.

Paulsen & Lutz. "Behavior Therapy for Weight Control: Long-Term Results of Two Programs." *American Journal of Clinical Nutrition*, 1976, 29, pp.880–888.

Paulsen & Beneke. "Long-Term Results from a Weight Loss Program." *Journal of Nutrition Education*, 1979,11(1), pp. 42–45.

Pearce & Dayton. "Incidence of Cancer in Men on a Diet High in Polyunsaturated Fat." *Lancet*, 1971, 1, pp.464–467.

Phillips, R. L. "Role of Lifestyle and Dietary Habits in Risk of Cancer Among 7th-day Adventists." *Cancer Research*, 1975, pp.3513–3522.

Pitt & Costrini. "Vitamin C Prophylaxis in Marine Recruits." *Journal of the American Medical Assoc.*, 1979,241, pp.908–914.

Sacks and Others. "Blood Pressure in Vegetarians." *American Journal of Epidemiology*, 1974, 100, pp.390–398.

Schachtele, Charles F. "Bacteria, Diet and the Prevention of Dental Caries." *Contemporary Nutrition*, Aug., 1980.

Seeman & Riggs. "Dietary Prevention of Bone Loss in the Elderly." *Geriatrics*, 1981,36(9), pp.71–79.

Shultz, P. "Walking for Rehabilitation: The First Step." *Physician and Sports Medicine*, 1980, 8, pp.109–112.

Skillman, T. G. "Can Osteoporosis Be Prevented?" *Geriatrics* 1980,35(2), pp.95–99.

Smith, E. L. "Exercise for Prevention of Osteoporosis: A Review." *The Physician and Sportsmedicine*, 1982,10(3), pp.72–79.

Thompson, M. "Geriatric Nutrition." *Journal of the National Medical Assoc.*, 1980,72(8), pp.795–803.

Todhunter & Darby. "Guidelines for Maintaining Adequate Nutrition in Old Age." *Geriatrics* 1978,33(6), pp.49–56.

Vitale, J. J. "Impact of Nutrition on Immune Function." *Nutrition in Disease*, 1980, pp.3–24.

Weg, R. B. "Prolonged Mild Nutritional Deficiencies: Significance for Health Maintenance. *Journal of Nutrition for the Elderly*, 1980, 1(1), pp.3–22.

White, Philip. "Food Fadism." *Contemporary Nutrition*, Feb., 1979.

Wilber, J. A. "The Role of Diet in the Treatment of High Blood Pressure." *American Dietetic Assoc. Journal*, 1982, 80, pp.25–28.

Windsor, A. C. "Nutrition in the Elderly." *Practitioner*, 1979, 222, pp.625–629.

Winick, M. "Nutrition and Aging." *New York Journal of Medicine*, 1978, 78, pp.1970–1971.

Yearick & Others. "Nutritional Status of the Elderly: Biochemical and Dietary Findings." *Journal of Gerontology*, 1980, 35, pp.663–671.

ABOUT THE AUTHOR

Dr. Ann Tyndall has an earned doctorate in nutrition from the University of North Carolina at Greensboro. Her professional life has included university teaching, research, administration, radio and television appearances, and public speaking. She did her doctoral research on nutrition education methods for weight control and has helped over 1000 people to lose weight. Since that time, she has specialized in nutrition and the aging process and has done teaching at the graduate level, consulting with business and industry, private counseling, lectures and writing.

Dr. Ann Tyndall
Route 3, 19 Tamworth Drive
Clemmons, North Carolina 27409

(919) 764-5950